Learning Language Arts Through Literature

THE YELLOW
STUDENT ACTIVITY BOOK
3RD EDITION

By

Debbie Strayer

and

Susan Simpson

Common Sense Press
Simple to teach. Easy to learn.

The *Learning Language Arts Through Literature* series:

The Blue Book - 1st Grade Skills
The Red Book - 2nd Grade Skills
The Yellow Book - 3rd Grade Skills
The Orange Book - 4th Grade Skills
The Purple Book - 5th Grade Skills
The Tan Book - 6th Grade Skills
The Green Book - 7th Grade Skills
The Gray Book - 8th Grade Skills
The Gold Book - World Literature - High School Skills
The Gold Book - American Literature - High School Skills
The Gold Book - British Literature - High School Skills
The Gold Book – Literary Criticism - High School Skills

Our thanks to Debbie Ward for her work on the 3rd edition of this book.

Common Sense Press of Melbourne LLC
3121 Skyway Circle, Suite A
Melbourne, FL 32934
www.commonsensepress.com

Cover Design: Kate White, 2017
Cover art: Nongkran_ch/Bigstock.com

Printed in the United States of America.

Rev 05/2021

ISBN 978-1-929683-42-0

Message to the Student

Welcome to *Learning Language Arts Through Literature*! This is *The Yellow Student Activity Book* where you will record your answers to the questions from *The Yellow Teacher Book.*

You will enjoy learning language arts as you read good books and practice your writing skills in fun and creative ways. Remember, any skill seems difficult at first, but as you complete each day's work you will get better.

Throughout your *Student Book* you will find *Notes* pages. Use these pages for extra work, to practice your penmanship, or to take notes.

Enjoy yourself this year while *Learning Language Arts Through Literature.*

☆ ☆ ☆ ☆

Teacher's Note

The *Yellow Student Activity Book* is a companion to the *The Yellow Teacher Book* from the *Learning Language Arts Through Literature* series. There are 36 numbered lessons with each lesson divided into 5 days. The average time for one lesson is five days. At the completion of the 36 lessons, your student will accomplish 180 days of work.

For example, Lesson 1 consists of Days 1-5. On Day 1 your student completes a.- d.:
a) listen, copy literature passage, make corrections, etc.
b) punctuation - periods and commas
c) copy spelling words and discuss spelling patterns
d) optional enrichment

The following day you would teach Day 2, a.- f. Typically a student may need more time on certain skills while he moves quickly through others.

This book can not be used independently. It is designed to be used with its companion, *The Yellow Teacher Book* which contains the complete teaching material, information, and answers you need to teach the program. *The Yellow Teacher Book* and other products by Common Sense Press can be found at the Common Sense Press web site: ***www.commonsensepress.com.***

Table of Contents

EVERYDAY WORDS

That wood was full of rabbit holes. In the neatest, sandiest hole of all lived Benjamin's aunt and his cousins Flopsy, Mopsy, Cotton-tail, and Peter. Mrs. Rabbit earned her living by knitting rabbit wool mittens and scarves.

The Tale of Benjamin Bunny by Beatrix Potter, 1904

Day 1 a. Copy the sentences. Compare your copy to the literature passage and make corrections.

b. There are three (3) **periods** in this passage. Circle each one. There are four (4) **commas** in this passage. Draw a square around each one. Read the passage to your teacher paying attention to periods and commas.

Focus on Spelling

knot know knife knock knee

Bonus Word: because

c. Copy these spelling words. Say the words aloud as you write them.

d. Enrichment

Find the spelling words in this puzzle. They are read down or across.

Circle the words: knot knee know knife knock

w	m	k	n	o	w	b
n	a	n	o	v	e	k
i	f	o	g	e	t	n
h	t	t	a	r	o	o
k	n	e	e	n	d	c
k	n	i	f	e	v	k

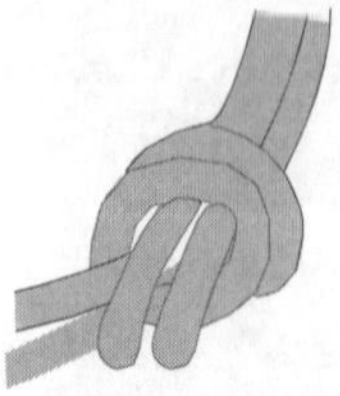

Day 2 a. Discussion with teacher.

boy girl city month love

Grammar Guide
Noun - person, place, thing, or idea

b.

Grammar Guide
Proper noun - name of a particular person, place, or thing. Proper nouns are spelled with a capital letter.

Make a list of the people in your family.

c. Using the sentences you copied yesterday underline the words that start with capital letters and are *not* at the beginning of a sentence.

d. Why do you think the words you underlined start with capital letters?

e. Orally make up a sentence for each of the common nouns in **2a**, then re place the nouns with proper nouns.

f. **SEE-SPELL-SAY:** Look and **see** each word on the spelling list. **Spell** each word aloud. **Say** the word.

Day 3 a. Looking in the literature passage find a word that begins with a silent letter and circle that word.

b. Discussion with teacher.

Phonics Fact
kn at the beginning of a word says /**n**/.

c. knot know knew knee knife knock

d. Cross out the **k** to show it is silent, like this: ~~k~~nife

e. Use the words to fill in the blanks for these sentences:

knot know knee knife knock

1) Mom will cut the cake with a ________________.

2) I ________________ God loves me.

3) The boy fell off his bike and hurt his ________________.

4) When the mailman brings my box he will ________________ on the door.

5) Dad will tie a ________________ in the rope so we can swing on it.

f. Spelling Bee

Day 4 a. Discussion with teacher.

b. Discussion with teacher.

Punctuation Pointer
Period - (.) ends a telling sentence

Two things are wrong with this telling sentence. Tell your teacher how to correct it.

the rabbit ran to the barn

c. Correct these sentences.

1) my mother is going to the store

2) the car is red and very old

3) we get up at seven o'clock in the morning

4) the bears at the zoo look hungry

5) a big cat is sitting in the yard

d. Choose a book you like to read. Show your teacher at least two telling sentences.

e. Spelling Pretest

Day 5 a. Looking at the literature passage from Day 1, how did Benjamin find his aunt's rabbit hole in a wood filled with rabbit holes?

b. Use your imagination: Write three sentences describing Mrs. Rabbit's home. You may include information about her children and her work.

c. Spelling Test

d. Enrichment

Some words are big and some words are little.

Write the shortest word you know. ______________

Write the longest word you know. ______________

e. Handwriting

This year you learn cursive writing. It may seem hard at first, but in a short time you will write sentences with no problems. Cursive writing is fun and helpful. You can write faster in cursive.

To write in cursive, remember three things:

1. Sit up straight, but comfortably, in your chair.
2. Place your writing paper on a slant.
3. Hold your pen or pencil correctly.

Review Activities

1. Circle all the proper nouns in the lists below.

a. Tom	boy	come	today
b. girl	Nancy	city	Tampa
c. building	Maple Street	Lincoln Center	church

2. Rewrite each sentence adding capitalization and punctuation.

   a. we went to the zoo

   ____

   ____

   b. the doctor is late

   ____

   ____

   c. a big dog ran through our yard

   ____

   ____

   d. they will bring the cake

   ____

   ____

3. Write a telling sentence using one of your spelling words.

   ____

   ____

Notes

Peter was sitting by himself. He looked poorly and was dressed in a red cotton pocket handkerchief.

"Peter, who has your clothes?" said Little Benjamin, in a whisper.

Peter replied, "The scarecrow in Mr. McGregor's garden."

The Tale of Benjamin Bunny by Beatrix Potter, 1904

Day 1. a. Copy the first two sentences. Compare your copy to the literature passage and make corrections.

b. Look at the passage for this lesson. Underline the words between the quotation marks in the last sentence. Ask someone to read the quotes with you.

Focus on Spelling

every everybody everyone everything everywhere

Bonus Word: clothes

c. Copy these spelling words. Say the words aloud as you write them.

______________________ ______________________

______________________ ______________________

______________________ ______________________

d. Enrichment

Unscramble these letters to make your spelling words.

1) eeryv ________________ 4) eebdoyrvy ________________

2) reeeewvyhr ________________ 5) eegynrvhti ________________

3) eeeonrvy ________________

Day 2 a. Underline the word that tells how Peter looked when Benjamin found him.

b. Substitute the words *not well* for *poorly*. Does it change the meaning of the sentence?.

Grammar Guide

Synonym - a word of similar meaning

c. Discussion with teacher.

Using Your Tools

thesaurus is a book of synonyms listed in alphabetical order.

d. Practice using your thesaurus by looking up the word *big*. Copy at least three synonyms for the word *big*.

______________ ______________ ______________

e. Using a thesaurus pick three words from our literature passage and find a synonym, or a word with a close meaning, for each of your words. Make a sentence using each word. Try your synonym in its place. Did it mean the same thing?

f. **SEE-SPELL-SAY:** Look and **see** each word on the spelling list. **Spell** each word aloud. **Say** the word.

Day 3 a. Discussion with teacher.

looking: look **-ing**

b. Discussion with teacher.

Grammar Guide
To add the suffix **-ing** or **-ed** to a word ending in silent **e**, first drop the **e**, and then add the suffix. Ex: bake - baking, baked

Grammar Guide
To add the suffix **-ing** or **-ed** to a one syllable word ending with a short vowel and a consonant, double the last consonant, and then add the suffix. Ex: stop - stopping, stopped

c. The suffix **-ing** has been added to a word in the literature passage. Circle the word with a red pencil.

d. Add the suffixes **-ing** and **-ed** to these words.
Ex: bake baking baked

1) joke ____________ ____________

2) care ____________ ____________

3) hike ____________ ____________

4) race ____________ ____________

Ex: stop stopping stopped

5) jog ______________ ______________

6) pat ______________ ______________

7) hop ______________ ______________

8) clap ______________ ______________

e. Spelling Bee

Day 4 a. Read these examples to your teacher.

out + side = outside side + walk = sidewalk
cup + cake = cupcake base + ball = baseball

Grammar Guide
Compound Word - two words joined together to make a new word

b. There is a compound word in our literature passage. Find it and underline it with a colored pencil. Draw a line between the two words that have been joined together.

c. Discussion with teacher.

d. Read these compound words. Draw a line between the two words that have been joined together.

mailman everywhere football bedroom birthday

e. Use the list of compound words you just divided to fill in these sentences.

1) I will be nine years old on my ______________.

2) My father and I like to play ______________.

3) We looked ______________ for our lost dog.

4) The ______________ puts letters in the box by the road.

5) My ______________ is a good place to play and sleep.

f. Spelling Pretest

______________________ ______________________

______________________ ______________________

______________________ ______________________

Day 5 a. Discussion with teacher.

b. Spelling Test

______________________ ______________________

______________________ ______________________

______________________ ______________________

c. Enrichment

Fill in the blanks using a word that begins with **st**.

Ex: Instead of go, I <u>stop</u>.

1) I sit on the chair and I ____________ on the floor.

2) To finish something I must first ____________.

3) At night I can see the moon and the ____________.

Fill in the blanks using a word that begins with **br**.

Ex: The <u>bride</u> and groom were happy.

4) I will sweep the floor with a ____________.

5) Be careful not to ____________ the window.

6) The dentist wants me to ____________ my teeth after every meal.

d. Handwriting

Review Activities

1. Write a synonym for each word.

   a. big ______________ c. look ______________

   b. little ______________ d. run ______________

2. Add the suffix **-ing** to these words.

   a. take ______________ d. care ______________

   b. win ______________ e. bite ______________

   c. run ______________ f. stop ______________

3. Circle the compound words.

   mailman bedroom

   enough birthday

   everywhere water

4. Write a proper noun for each common noun listed below:

   a. boy ______________ c. street ______________

   b. cat ______________ d. girl ______________

Notes

For the first time Mark started to feel really worried, not just about Grandma and the lighthouse, but about Carol herself. He went back to the shop but the shopkeeper hadn't seen her.

The Other Kitten by Patricia St. John.
Used by permission, 1984, Bethany House Publishers.

Day 1 a. Copy the sentences. Compare your copy to the literature passage and make corrections.

b.

Focus on Spelling

feel keep wheel seen need

Bonus Word: really

Copy these spelling words. Say the words aloud as you write them.

c. Enrichment

Fill in the blanks with your spelling words.

1) 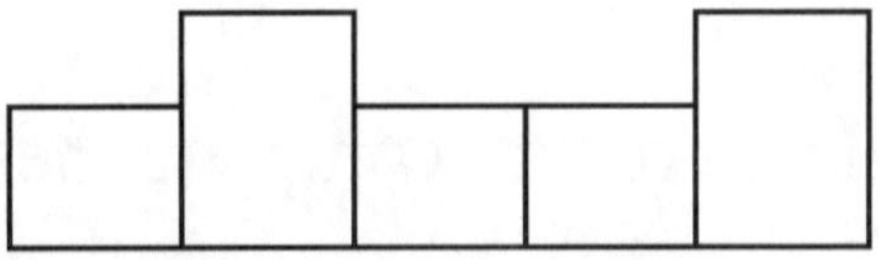

2) 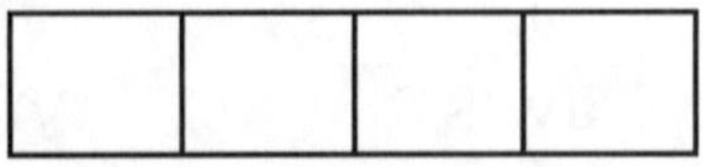

3) 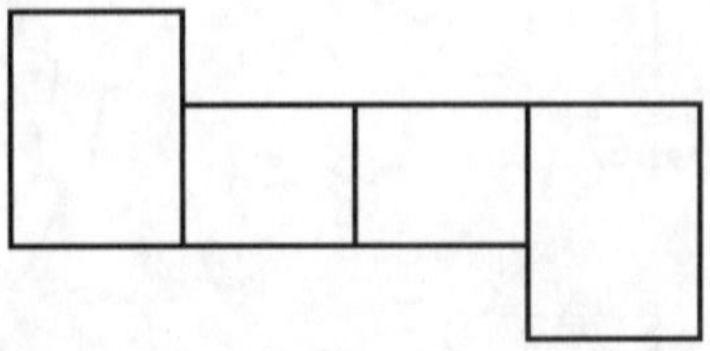

4) 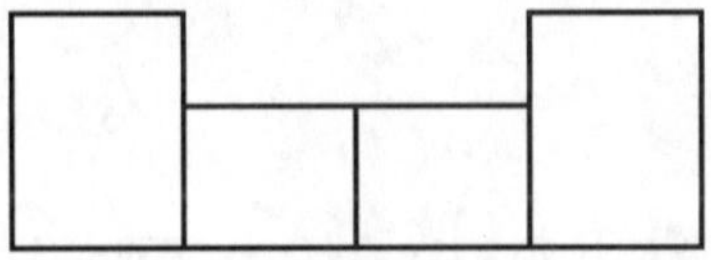

5) 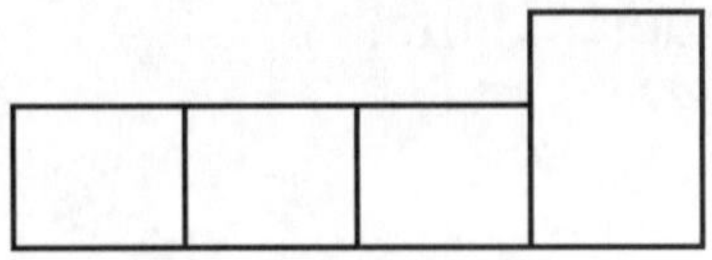

Day 2 a. Discussion with teacher.

b. Find the compound words in our literature passage and underline them.

c. Can you think of any other compound words that include these words? (The words may be used as the first or second part of the word.)

light	house	self

d. Write sentences using the compound words from your list.

e. **SEE-SPELL-SAY:** Look and **see** each word on the spelling list. **Spell** each word aloud. **Say** the word.

f. Enrichment

Think of nouns, or naming words, to complete these sentences.

1) The ________________ flies.

2) The ________________ crawls.

3) The ________________ bounces.

4) The ________________ roars.

5) The ________________ speaks.

6) The ________________ cooks.

Day 3 a. The suffix, or ending, **-ed** has been added to two words in our literature passage. Find these words and underline them.

b. Discussion with teacher.

Grammar Guide
When adding the suffix **-ed** to words ending in a consonant and **y**, first change the **y** to **i**, and then add **-ed**. Ex: worry - worried

Add **-ed** to these words.

1) try ________________ 3) carry ________________

2) hurry ________________ 4) empty ________________

c. Use the words you made in the last section to fill in these blanks:

1) Dad ______________________ the bags into the house.

2) Mom said we were late, so we all __________ to get dressed.

3) The wheel kept falling off my wagon, so I __________ to fix it.

4) The trash was full, so my brother __________________ it.

d. Spelling Bee

Day 4 a. – b. Discussion with teacher.

c. There are examples of cause and effect in our daily lives. Look at these effects, and think of possible causes:

1) Your sister or brother is crying. ____________________

____

2) My mother and father are very happy. ____________________

____

3) There is a warm meal on the table. ____________________

____

4) You have a new shirt or dress to wear. ____________________

____

d. Discussion with teacher. Think of an event, person, or feeling that made you worry. Write at least three sentences telling about this situation. In the fourth sentence tell how the situation turned out. Remember to begin your sentences with a capital letter and end with a period.

____

____

____

____

e. Spelling Pretest

5. a. Listen to your teacher read the vocabulary words.

Vocabulary

seashore	different	seagulls	castle
wonderful	animals	wind	enough
smooth	shovel	quiet	listen

b. Read the story "The Seashore" to your teacher.

The Seashore

The seashore is a wonderful place to visit where you can find neat things to look at and fun things to do. Many seashores have sand where the water meets the land which is called a beach. Some beaches have sand that is soft and fun to play in. If you have a shovel you can dig a hole or build a castle in the sand.

The sea comes up to the shore in waves. Sometimes the wind makes the waves very big, and other times, the waves are smooth and quiet. If it is warm enough people swim in the sea. Some people like to float if the waves are not too rough.

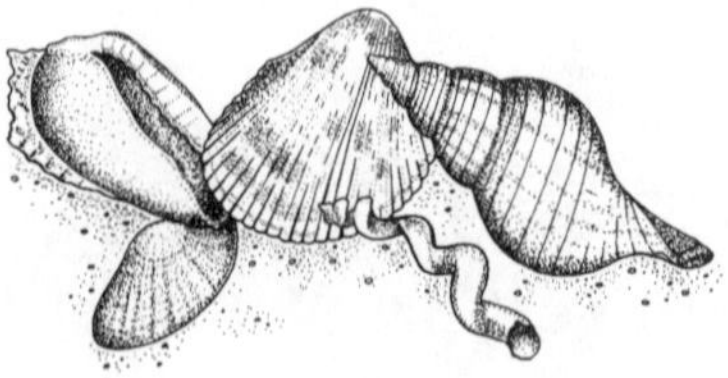

Many different things live at the seashore. Fish are found in the sea water. Some animals swim in the water. Other animals, like crabs, crawl on the sand. Some animals, like seagulls, can walk on the sand, float in the water, or fly in the air. There always seems to be something moving at the seashore.

When you come to the seashore look for pretty shells. Try to catch a wave as it comes up on the sand. Listen to birds call to each other and dive for fish. Then you can tell your own seashore story.

c. Discussion Questions

1) What is the sandy place called where the water meets the land?

2) What can you do in the sand?

3) What kind of animals live at the seashore?

d. Spelling Test

__________ __________

__________ __________

__________ __________

e. Enrichment

Read the word on the left, and then read the sentence. By changing only the first letter, complete the sentence with a new word.

Ex: bunny The clown was <u>funny</u>.

1) cup A baby dog is called a __________.

2) hump A garbage site is called a __________.

3) lake Mom will __________ some cookies.

f. Handwriting

Review Activities

1. Add the suffix **-ed** to the following words.

   a. worry ____________

   b. carry ____________

   c. bury ____________

   d. empty ____________

2. Circle the proper nouns.

Lucy	house	store
dog	Food Mart	Aunt Sally

3. Rewrite each sentence adding capitalization and punctuation.

   a. the car is clean now ____________________

   ____

   b. that cat is pretty ____________________

   ____

   c. we went to the store ____________________

   ____

4. Add the suffix **-ing** to these words.

   a. hop ____________

   b. stop ____________

   c. fake ____________

   d. move ____________

He looked up at her and saw that her eyes were shut like when she prayed at night, and he knew that she was praying for Carol.

The Other Kitten by Patricia St. John.
Used by permission, 1984,
Bethany House Publishers.

Day 1 a. Copy the sentence. Compare your copy to the literature passage and make corrections.

b. 

Focus on Spelling

pray crayon holiday gray stay

Bonus Word: were

Copy these spelling words. Say the words aloud as you write them.

c. Enrichment

Find your spelling words in this puzzle: pray gray crayon holiday stay

w	s	f	g	o	m	b
i	t	p	r	a	y	a
t	f	q	a	e	t	l
c	r	a	y	o	n	o
b	e	s	t	a	y	n
h	o	l	i	d	a	y

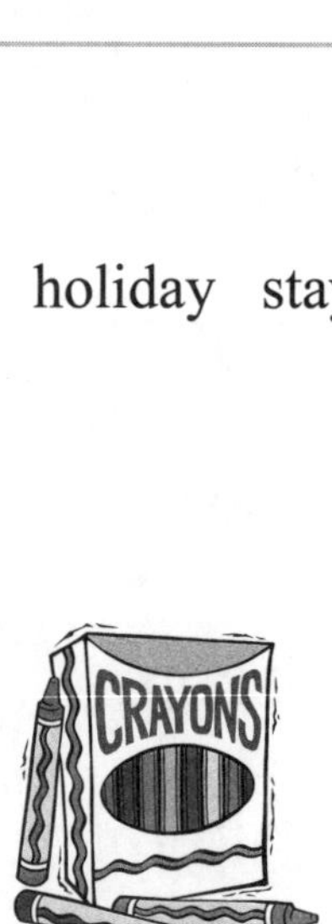

d. Review the spelling words from Lessons 1 – 3.

Day 2 a. One of the words in our literature passage has two letters in the middle of the word that are silent. Circle the word.

b. What sounds do we hear in the word *night*? Cross out the two silent letters in the word *night*.

night

Phonics Fact
When **gh** follows **i** the **gh** is silent, and **i** says /**i**/.

c. Make as many words as you can by adding one or two letters to the beginning of these letters:
Ex: bright ________ight

________ ________ ________

________ ________ ________

________ ________ ________

Show your teacher and read the words to her.

d. Read the following list of words to your teacher.

flight night fight slight right

Use these words to complete the following sentences:

1) He writes with his ________________ hand.

2) If you don't stop them, the dog and cat will ________________.

3) The boy fell from a low chair, so his bump is ________________.

4) The stars are pretty at ________________.

5) Our ________________ to Grandma's house leaves at ten o'clock.

e. **SEE-SPELL-SAY:** Look and **see** each word on the spelling list. **Spell** each word aloud. **Say** the word.

Day 3 a. Tell your teacher the proper nouns in these sentences:

1) Bob lives in a big house in New York.
2) My brother Jack is in town.
3) He likes to go to Disney World.

b. Look back at the literature passages for Lessons 2, 3, and 4. Make a list of the proper nouns used in these lessons.

____________ ____________ ____________

____________ ____________ ____________

____________ ____________ ____________

c. Make up three sentences using these proper nouns:

1) a particular person's name

____

____

2) a particular place's name

____

____

3) a particular thing's name

____

____

d. Spelling Bee

e. Enrichment

Fill in the blanks using a word that begins with **cl**.

Ex: I saw a funny <u>clown</u> at the circus.

1) There were pretty white ____________ in the blue sky.

2) The teacher praised the students in her ____________.

Fill in the blanks using a word that begins with **tr**.

Ex: The hunter set up a <u>trap</u>.

3) I taught my dog some ____________.

4) Mom sat in the shade under the big ____________.

5) Dad likes to fish for ____________.

Day 4 a. Discussion with teacher.

Grammar Guide

To add the suffix **-ing** to words ending in **y**, just add **-ing**.

Ex: play - playing worry - worrying

b. Add the suffix **-ing** to the end of these words. Write the new words you made.
Ex: play playing

1) say ____________ 5) try ____________

2) pay ____________ 6) hurry ____________

3) stay ____________ 7) carry ____________

4) play ____________ 8) empty ____________

c. Discussion with teacher.

Grammar Guide

When adding the suffix **-ed** and **-ing** to all other words, just add the suffix.

Ex: help - helped - helping
leak - leaked - leaking

d. Add **-ed** and **-ing** to the end of these words. Write the new words you have made.

Ex: help helped helping

1) ask ______________ ______________

2) need ______________ ______________

3) wash ______________ ______________

4) peel ______________ ______________

5) paint ______________ ______________

6) call ______________ ______________

e. You have a list of eight words with suffixes from exercise **4b**. Use some of these words to fill in the blanks in these sentences.

1) Mary is ______________ with her cousin.

2) The men are ______________ heavy boxes.

3) My aunt is ______________ with us.

4) I am ______________ to learn to ride a bike.

5) My neighbor is ______________ me to walk his dog.

f. Spelling Pretest

______________ ______________

______________ ______________

______________ ______________

Day 5 a. Write the passage from dictation. Compare your writing to the passage and make corrections.

____

____

____

____

____

____

b. Discussion with teacher.

c. Spelling Test

______________________ ______________________

______________________ ______________________

______________________ ______________________

d. Enrichment

The words in each list share one letter in common.
What letter is it?

1)	simple	drive	fight	___	4)	chance	shin	only	___
2)	laugh	grow	hinge	___	5)	Billy	Jenny	Tommy	___
3)	beep	forest	garden	___	6)	loose	comb	goat	___

e. Handwriting

e e

l l

a c

o d

i t

Review Activities

1. Add the suffix **-ing** to these words ending in **y**.

   a. stay ____________________

   b. carry ____________________

   c. try ____________________

   d. say ____________________

2. Add the suffix **-ing** and **-ed** to these words.

	-ing	**-ed**
a. ask	________	________
b. yell	________	________
c. talk	________	________
d. peel	________	________

3. Circle the compound words

mailman everyone carpenter today someone doctor

4. Rewrite each sentence adding capitalization and punctuation.

   a. ryan likes to go to the movies

   ____

   b. can you take care of my dog, lucy

   ____

   c. i wish i could go with you to the park

   ____

dictionary: noun dic tion ar y \dik shon air ee\
plural: dictionaries
1: a reference source in print or electronic form containing words usually listed alphabetically along with information about their forms, pronunciations, and meanings
2: a reference book listing alphabetically terms or names important to a particular subject such as a medical dictionary
3: a reference book listing alphabetically the words of one language and showing their meanings in another language
4: a computerized list used for reference

Day 1 a. This entry is taken from the Merriam-Webster Dictionary online. Read the entry with your teacher.

b – d. Discussion with teacher.

e. Write the following words in the first column.

lizard dog fish cat pig

______________	______________
______________	______________
______________	______________
______________	______________
______________	______________

Place a piece of paper over the words covering all but the first letters. Say the alphabet out loud **a - b - c**...There are no words that begin with the letters **a** or **b**. but the word *cat* begins with the letter **c**. Write *cat* in the second column. Continue saying the alphabet and writing the word that comes next in alphabetical order.

f. Enrichment

Think of nouns, or naming words, to complete these sentences.

1) The ______________ whistles.

2) The ______________ sings.

3) The ______________ plays.

4) The ______________ barks.

5) The ______________ hops.

6) The ______________ shouts.

Day 2 a. Discussion with teacher.

b. Write a sentence using the word *wallaby*.

____

c. Discussion with teacher.

d. Write a sentence using the word *gecko*.

____

e. Write the plural form for *wallaby* and *gecko*.

__________________ __________________

f. Look at these words:

apple able all ant

Cover the first letter of each word and put them in order by the second letter.

____

____

____

____

g. Enrichment

Which items go together? Draw a line from one column to the other.

Ex: bat ——— baseball

1) boat	spoon
2) plate of meat	tennis ball
3) bowl of soup	oar
4) tennis racquet	fork
5) paper	pencil

Day 3 a. – h. Discussion with teacher.
Play the Dictionary Game.

Day 4 a. Discussion with teacher.

b. Put these words in alphabetical order.

apply apple

____

____

c. Put these words in alphabetical order.

work would wood

____

____

____

d. You have been introduced to spelling words in Lessons 1 – 4. Review these words, as well as any words you may have added to the list as your personal spelling words.

e. Enrichment

Fill in the blanks using a word that begins with **pl**.

1) Everybody should say ________________ and thank you.

2) After I do my work, I can ________________.

3) I like peaches and ________________.

Fill in the blanks using a word that begins with **dr**.

4) My brother is learning how to ________________ a car.

5) Mom hangs out the clothes to ________________.

6) My sister plays the piano, and I play the ________________.

Day 5 a. Spelling

b. Dictation

c. Discussion with teacher.

d. Handwriting

Review Activities

Choose the skills your student needs.

1. Using a dictionary, find the part of speech for each word

.

   a. rough ______________________________

   b. tumble ______________________________

   c. change ______________________________

   d. testimony ______________________________

2. Put the following words in alphabetical order.

   panda elephant tiger swan

   ____

3. Put these words in alphabetical order.

   rodeo radio radius ratio

   ____

4. Fill in the blanks with these words. Use your dictionary if needed.

   wonder member humble pretend

   a. Even though he is the best player on the team, he is still ________________.

   b. I sometimes ________________ if my dog thinks of me when I am gone.

   c. He is a ____________________ of the baseball team.

   d. My sister likes to __________________ she is a teacher.

Assessment 1

(Lessons 1 – 5)

1. Rewrite these sentences adding capitalization and punctuation.

   a. she was late for the party ______________________________

   ____

   b. he went to the store __________________________________

   ____

   c. we like cake ______________________________________

2. Circle the proper nouns.

   girl boy Tom dog Main Street

3. Write a synonym for each word.

   a. big ______________________________

   b. little ______________________________

4. Adding the suffix **-ing** to these words.

   a. give ______________________________

   b. win ______________________________

   c. move______________________________

   d. stay ______________________________

   e. try ______________________________

   f. hop ______________________________

5. Add the suffix **-ed** to these words.

a. carry ______________________

b. clean ______________________

c. bury ______________________

6. Make two compound words using the word *every.*

______________________ ______________________

7. Put these words in alphabetical order.

a. apple ______________________

b. goat ______________________

c. about ______________________

d. how ______________________

Notes

LITERATURE LINK

Day 1 Listen to your teacher read the vocabulary words.

Vocabulary

Tilda	Tennessee	troublemaker	chicken
visitors	special	invited	outwit
enough	bridle	saddle	reins
different	comfortable		

Discussion with your teacher.

Begin reading the story "Tilda the Troublemaker." You will have time tomorrow to finish the story.

Tilda the Troublemaker

As a little girl, going to my grandpa's farm was the best trip. Mom, Dad, and I would drive to Grandpa's little town. We would leave on Friday, and it would take hours to get there. Riding in the car was fun because we ate chicken out of a box. Sometimes my mom would play games with me while we drove. Sometimes I would read or draw to pass the time; sometimes I would sleep. Finally we would get to the small town where my grandpa lived.

My grandpa's old farm was always a special place for me. He had lived there for many years. Grandma and Grandpa were always happy to see us, and they invited us to the best tasting dinners I ever ate. Chickens and cows were there as well as pecan and pear trees. All the things on the farm seemed wonderful. The one thing that was best though was Tilda.

Tilda was a Tennessee Walking Horse. This was funny because she didn't like to do much walking. A better name for her would have been a Tennessee Resting Horse. She lived there long before I first visited Grandpa's old farm. Tilda had been Grandpa's horse for a long time. She was a warm dark brown with a black tail and mane. Her face had a smart look to it as if she were trying to outwit the people around her. She had a white blaze on her head that made her look pretty.

If you came to see Tilda it was best to bring food — and lots of it. She would lift her head to look at visitors and then she would come if you held out your hand as if you had a snack. We would bring sugar cubes, which were her favorite, and carrots. Mom showed me how to feed her so I wouldn't get a bite from her big teeth. (Carrots and fingers can look alike.)

The best part of visiting Tilda was getting to ride her. While it was best for me it was not something she liked to do. If you weren't quick, like Grandpa, Tilda would run away when she saw the bridle. Grandpa would call her to come. They seemed to fuss at each other until the bridle was on. She would wait while he saddled her without too much fussing. I found that a sugar cube every now and then helped. Then she would be ready to ride.

Mom, Dad, or Grandpa would ride her first because sometimes she would show her temper. Then I would get to ride her. I had to hang on to the saddle horn. The world looked very different from Tilda's back. She seemed so tall, and I felt very tall as well. Until I was nine or so, someone always held the reins while I rode. Then I got to hold the reins sometimes but only for Tilda to walk around the farmyard.

Tilda was a very smart horse. She would think of ways to get a rider off her back. One time my dad was riding her in the pine forest. Tilda decided enough was enough. She turned and came trotting back to the barn. My dad talked to her and pulled on the reins, but Tilda didn't listen. Her sights were set on the barn. Soon he had a very big problem. Tilda was tall, and my dad was taller sitting on her. The barn door was much shorter than they were. Watching Tilda running into the barn with my dad ducking and yelling was a funny sight. I think even Tilda was laughing!

After a few years I got to ride Tilda around the farm by myself. She was getting older, but she didn't seem to be any fonder of riding. One day I was riding her in the pine forest. Do you know what happened? She decided she had had enough riding and off to the barn she went. She ran very closely to the trees to bump my legs. I stayed in the saddle. Then she tried a new trick on me. She ran towards a fence and jumped over it. I was so busy holding on that I don't remember much, but when we got back to the barn I started to fuss at her.

As I stood looking at her she snorted and stamped her foot. She seemed to be telling me what I already knew. She and Grandpa had an understanding. The two of them had been together a long time. Tilda felt comfortable with Grandpa on her back. She only let us ride her because we fed her sugar and carrots. I still think that Tilda liked going for those rides with the rest of us. She just had to tell us when enough was enough. To me she was a troublemaker. She was also the best horse ever.

Day 2 a. Finish reading the book or story from yesterday.

b. **Discussion Questions for *The White Stallion*:**

1) How many families are in the wagon train? Who is in Gretchen's family that is traveling west?
2) Who is Anna? Why did Father tie Gretchen to Anna's back?
3) When did Father and Mother discover that Gretchen was missing? What did they do then?
4) How do you think the family felt during the night? How did Gretchen feel?
5) Tell how the wild horses acted friendly to Anna. What did the horses do that frightened Gretchen?
6) What amazing thing did the white stallion do? Do you think he was trying to help Gretchen?
7) What did Mother tell her to do if she were ever lost? Did she obey Mother?
8) How did Gretchen get back to her family? Do you think the white stallion helped again?

Discussion Questions for "Tilda the Troublemaker":

1) Who is traveling to Grandpa's farm? Make a list of the people mentioned in the first paragraph.
2) Who is Tilda? Does the name of her kind of horse seem to fit her? Tell why or why not.
3) What did Tilda like best about visitors? Name her favorite snacks.
4) What did the little girl in the story like best about visiting Tilda?
5) Choose the word that best describes Tilda's temperament, or attitude:

   calm mean stubborn

6) Tell some of the ways Tilda would try to get riders off her back.
7) Tilda would let some people ride her, and then she would get tired of it and decide to go back to the barn. What sentence or phrase in the story best describes Tilda getting to this point? (Paragraphs 7 and 8)
8) How do you think the little girl really feels about Tilda? If you don't know read the last line of the story.

c. Look up these words in a dictionary and develop your horse vocabulary. You may just read them, or you may read them and write them down.

mustang	mare	stallion
colt	whinny	neigh
muzzle	nip	herd

Day 3 a. Discussion with teacher.

b. Here are some pictures of horses. Orally or in writing describe the horses in the pictures to your teacher. Use as many describing words as you can.

Here is an example:
The big dark horse has a beautiful, long mane.

Day 4 a. Here is a chart that shows the parts of a horse. Read the names of the parts to your teacher. You may want to color the horse or trace your own horse picture by placing white paper over the chart.

b. Fill in the sentence blanks with the correct parts.

mane muzzle flanks hoof tail

1) The hair on the horse's neck is called his ____________.
2) Often a horseshoe is put on a horse's ____________.
3) On summer days a horse will use his long ____________ to swish away flies.
4) The horse's nose and ____________ are very soft and sensitive.
5) The horse's strong ____________ help him run fast and work hard.

Day 5 a. To finish your study on horses tell your teacher about the horse you would like to have. You may use the following suggested questions:

1) What would you name your horse?
2) What would he or she look like? Remember to use the names of the horse parts and use describing words for your horse.
3) What would you do with your horse?
4) How would you feel about your horse?

b. After answering these questions write a sentence on the lines below to answer each question. (For example, "I will name my horse Flash.") After deciding what you will write make your final copy on the next page.

c.

Focus on Writing

A **paragraph** is a group of sentences that tell about one **main idea**. **Indent** the first sentence of a paragraph.

d. To complete your horse story you may want to draw a picture above your story that includes what you think your horse would look like. Share your story and picture with someone.

I **C.A.N.** Assessment
Literature Link on *Horses*

After the Literature Link on *Horses* is completed check off each I **C.A.N.** objective with your teacher.

_____	**C**	I can **complete** my work.
_____		I can be **creative**.
_____	**A**	I can be **accurate**.
_____		I can do my work with a good **attitude**.
_____	**N**	I can do my work **neatly**.

Notes

EVERYDAY WORDS

I want to learn to whistle.
I've always wanted to.
I fix my mouth to do it but
The whistle won't come through.

Day 1 a. Copy the poem from the model. Compare your copy to the model and make corrections.

b.

Focus on Spelling

through group mouth count ground

Bonus Word: always

Copy these spelling words. Say the words aloud as you write them.

c. Enrichment

Unscramble the letters to make your spelling words.

1) tonuc ________ 4) hghorut ________
2) utomh ________ 5) dgornu ________
3) gopur ________

Day 2 a.

Grammar Guide

Contractions - two words joined together with an apostrophe to replace missing letter(s)

Punctuation Pointer

Apostrophe - (') replaces missing letter(s) in a contraction

Read these words to your teacher, and write the words that make up the contractions. Tell your teacher which letters have been removed and replaced by an apostrophe:

1) isn't ________ 3) I'll ________
2) wasn't ________ 4) I'm ________

b. There are two contractions in the poem. Find them and underline them. What words were combined to make these contractions?

________ ________

c. Here is a list of commonly used contractions. Make up sentences orally using each contraction.

I + have = I've
can + not = can't
will + not = won't
did + not = didn't

I + will = I'll
do + not = don't
is + not = isn't
are + not = aren't

d. Underline the contraction in each sentence. Copy each sentence taking out the contraction and replacing it with the two words that make up the contraction.

1) I'll have more cake.

____

2) Dad can't find his hammer.

____

3) The book isn't on the table.

____

4) Mom didn't cook dinner tonight.

____

5) We aren't ready for winter.

____

6) We don't need to get a new car.

____

e. Discussion with teacher.

f. **SEE-SPELL-SAY:** Look and **see** each word on the spelling list. **Spell** each word aloud. **Say** the word.

Day 3 a. The word *whistle* ends in the letters **-le**. Read the following words aloud to your teacher. Tell what sound **-le** makes.

table people paddle turtle waffle gurgle

b. Divide the list of words from **3a** into syllables by drawing a line between the two syllables.

Phonics Fact

The letters **-le** at the end of a word will usually form its own syllable with the consonant before it.

c. Use the list of words from **3a** to fill in these sentence blanks:

1) While crossing the lake in the boat he lost the ________________.
2) I had eggs and a ________________ for breakfast.
3) Many ________________ came to the party.
4) Please come and set the ________________.
5) The green ________________ swam around the lake.
6) The water made a sound like a ________________.

d. Spelling Bee

e. Enrichment

Read the list of words. Circle the word that does not belong in the group.

Ex: dog cat bird (book)
This is a list of animals and *book* is not an animal.

1) Sam boy Justin Ronnie
2) Rome Paris city London
3) Saturn Mars Mercury planet
4) Tuesday Thursday week Saturday
5) February month August September
6) California Florida state Michigan

Day 4 a. On the first column write the first names of six friends.
On the second column rewrite the names in alphabetical order.

b. Look at this pattern: *Smith, Ann.*

Many times names are written with the last name first and the first name last. Write your name following this pattern.

c. Rewrite your list from **4a** following the pattern of last name first, then a comma, then first name. Put your list in alphabetical order by the last names.

d. Discussion with teacher.

e. Spelling Pretest

f. Enrichment

Read the list of words, and circle the word that does not belong in the group.

1) happy glad sad joyful

2) big tiny huge large

3) pretty nice pleasant bad

4) arms car legs hands

5) walk smell taste hear

6) run jog skip sit

Day 5 a. Discussion with teacher.

b. Make a list of the reasons people might whistle. The items on the list do not have to be complete sentences. Number your list, and put a period after each number.

c. This verse tells about wanting to be able to do something yet not being able to do it. Write a paragraph of three or four sentences telling about something you want to do but can't. Please include how you feel about it. Everyone has things he can't do. Remember to capitalize the first word of every sentence and end with a period. Indent the first sentence of the paragraph.

d. Spelling Test

e. Enrichment

Read the list of words, and circle the word that does not belong in the group.

1) chair couch table sofa

2) fork cup mug glass

3) build destroy make create

4) D E f G

5) unhappy sad gloomy joyful

6) branches grow roots trunk

f. Journal Entry: Write and/or draw pictures about a skill you want to learn.

g. Handwriting

m m

n n

i t

e l

u s

Review Activities

1. List the two words that make up the contractions.

   a. isn't ____________________

   b. don't ____________________

   c. can't ____________________

   d. I'll ____________________

2. Divide the words into syllables.

   a. table ____________________

   b. turtle ____________________

   c. little ____________________

   d. paddle ____________________

3. List the names in alphabetical order.

   Emily ____________________

   Ann ____________________

   Dan ____________________

   Megan ____________________

4. Divide these compound words. Example: every/day

   a. somewhere ____________________

   b. everyone ____________________

   c. today ____________________

   d. someday ____________________

I think perhaps it's stuck, and so
I try it once again.
Can people swallow whistles?
Where is my whistle then?

Day 1 a. Copy the poem from the model. Compare your copy to the model and make corrections.

b.

Focus on Spelling

yellow swallow follow pillow shadow

Bonus Word: perhaps

Copy these spelling words. Say the words aloud as you write them.

c. Enrichment
Fill in the blanks with letters to make your spelling words.

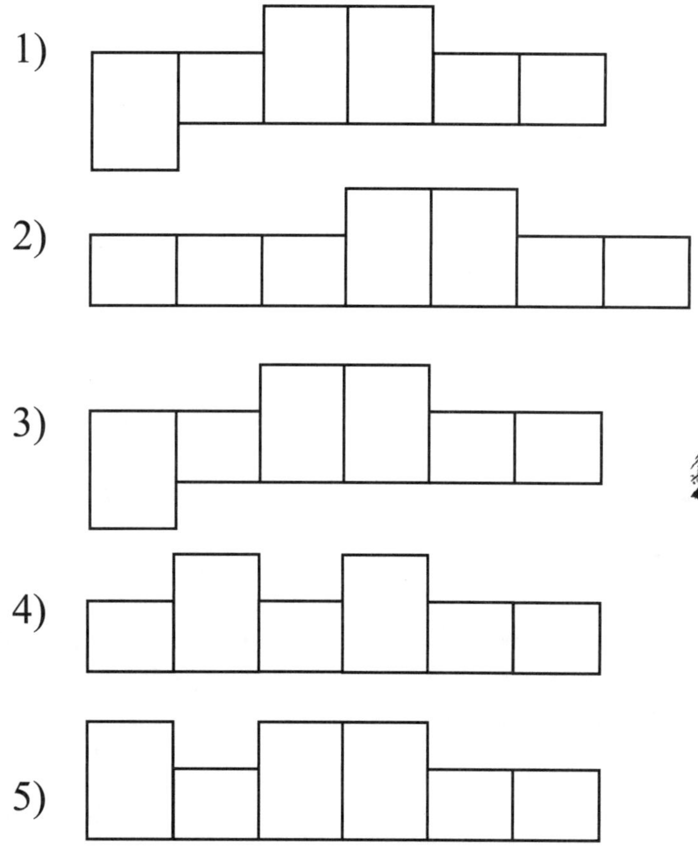

Day 2 a. Sometimes a word can have more than one meaning. Can you find a word in your verse that is both an object and an action? Circle the word.

b. The word *swallow* has more than one meaning. Look up this word in the dictionary and write two definitions (or meanings).

____

____

____

____

c. Here are some other words that have more than one meaning. Read the list to your teacher, and tell her the meanings you know for each word. Look up the words in a dictionary if you can't think of more than one meaning for them.

bank duck bat top

d. Use the words from **2c** to fill in these sentence blanks.

1) When we need money we go to the ______________________.

2) The ______________________ is swimming in the water.

3) The park is on the ______________________ of the river.

4) If you are tall sometimes you have to ______________ your head.

5) The boy watched the ______________________ spin around.

6) She hit the ball with the ______________________.

7) I climbed to the ______________________ of the ladder.

8) I saw a ______________________ fly into a cave.

e. **SEE-SPELL-SAY:** Look and **see** each word on the spelling list. **Spell** each word aloud. **Say** the word.

Day 3 a. There is a contraction in our verse. Find it, and underline it. What two words went together to make this contraction?

______________ ______________

b. Here is how you make this contraction: it + is = it's. Read this list of words, and tell your teacher how you think these contractions should be spelled:

1) he + is = ______________

2) she + is = ______________

3) you + are = ______________

4) I + am = ______________

5) we + are = ______________

6) they + are = ______________

c. Rewrite the sentences below and replace the words in italics with a contraction made in **3b.** Remember to start each sentence with a capital letter.

1) *She is* going to the park. ______________________

____

2) *They are* waiting for the bus. ______________________

____

3) *I am* making dinner. ______________________

____

4) *We are* driving to Grandma's house. ______________________

____

5) *You are* not the last one in line. ______________________

____

6) *He is* running to first base. ______________________

____

d. Look in a favorite book and find some contractions. Make a list of at least five contractions. Show the list to your teacher, and tell her what words were put together to make each contraction.

____

____

____

____

____

____

e. Spelling Bee

f. Enrichment

Read the list of words, and circle the word that does not belong in the group.

1) clams shrimp oyster sand

2) island ocean lake river

3) fly pelican sparrow crow

4) night light bite right

5) Susan girl Tracy Sandy

6) red blue purple bright

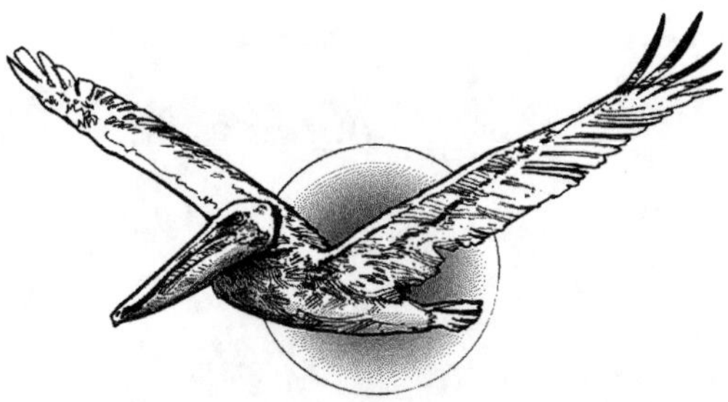

Day 4

a. In our verse there is a word that means the same as *maybe*. This word is a synonym, or a word close in meaning, to the word *maybe*. Underline the word.

b. Discussion with teacher.

c. Look up the following words in a thesaurus, and choose two synonyms for each word. (Remember, the thesaurus is arranged in alphabetical order like a dictionary.)

1) big ______________________

2) went ______________________

3) good ______________________

4) said ______________________

d. Rewrite the sentences using one of your synonyms in place of the word in italics.

1) The horse *went* back to the barn.

____

____

2) This birthday cake tastes *good*.

____

____

3) Mother *said*, "It is time to come in."

____

____

4) The *big* dog jumped into the car.

____

____

e. Spelling Pretest

f. Enrichment

Read the list of words, and circle the word that does not belong in the group.

1) run shoes sandals boots

2) milk eat juice tea

3) ocean lake pool catch

4) turtle lizard bunny snake

5) throw nice kind gentle

6) small horse little tiny

Day 5. a. Discussion with teacher.

b. Think of something that you kept trying to do and then were able to do. Did you give up trying? Draw a picture or write several sentences that show how practice helped you.

c. – d. Discussion with teacher.

e. Spelling Test

f. Journal Entry: Write a story about a character who accomplishes a goal after trying many times.

g. Handwriting

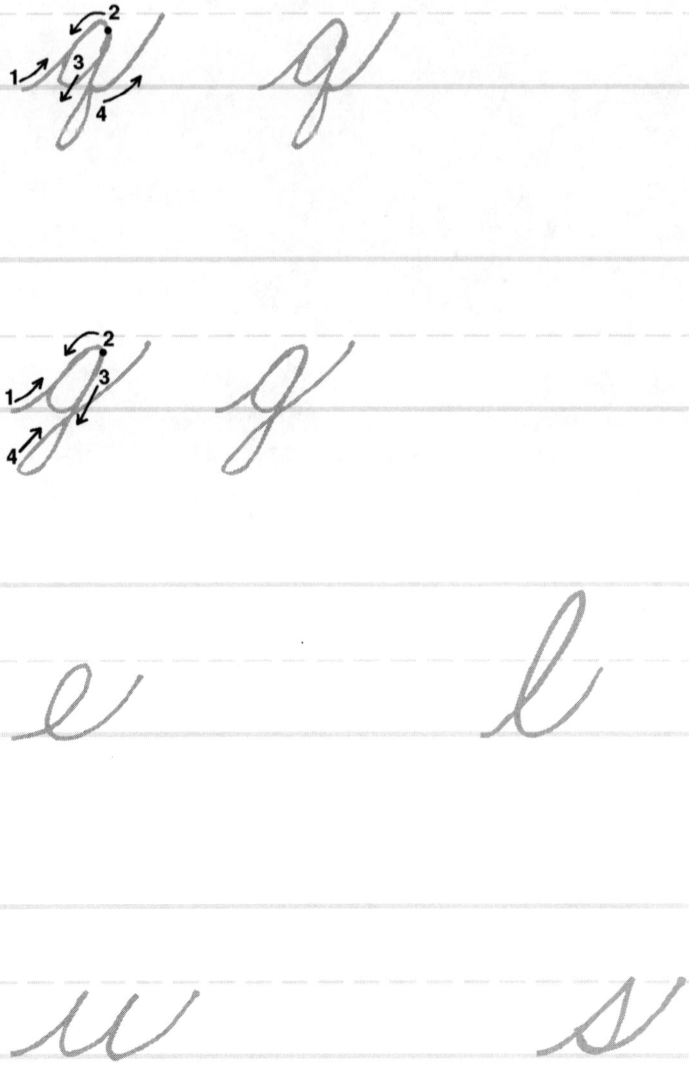

m n

Review Activities

1. Give two meanings for each word.

   a. bank ____________________

   ____

   b. bat ____________________

   ____

2. Write the contraction for each of these words.

   a. do not __________ d. we are __________

   b. it is __________ e. she is __________

   c. you arc __________ f. I am __________

3. Rewrite the sentences replacing the underlined words with a synonym.

   a. This sandwich is <u>good</u>. ____________________

   ____

   b. The <u>little</u> kitten climbed on me. ____________________

   ____

   c. We <u>went</u> to the fair. ____________________

   ____

4. List the words in alphabetical order.

   zebra monkey cheetah horse

   __________ __________ __________ __________

August 20, 2017

Dear Grandma and Grandpa,

How are you? We are all fine.
We went to the beach today. It was fun.
Billy and I found some small shells.
It was very hot. Please come to see us soon.

Love,
Ann

Day 1 a. Copy the letter. Compare your copy to the model and make corrections.

b.

Focus on Spelling

beach treat clean peace leave

Bonus Word: sincerely

Copy these spelling words. Say the words aloud as you write them.

______________ ______________ ______________

______________ ______________ ______________

c. Enrichment

Fill in the blank with the correct spelling word.

1) The opposite of dirty is ______________.

2) We build a sandcastle on the ______________.

3) The opposite of stay is ______________.

4) *Greet* rhymes with ______________.

5) The opposite of fighting is ______________.

d. Review the spelling words from lessons 7 – 8

Day 2 a. Discussion with teacher.

Focus on Writing

A **friendly letter** consists of a heading, greeting, body, closing, and signature.

b. Using different colored pencils or crayons, find and underline each part of the letter as it is named:
red – heading (or date)
blue – greeting (or saying hello)
yellow – draw a box around the body of the letter
green – closing (or saying goodbye)
orange – signature (or name of person writing the letter)

c. – d. Discussion with teacher.

e. **SEE-SPELL-SAY:** Look and **see** each word on the spelling list. **Spell** each word aloud. **Say** the word.

Day 3 a. In our letter there are two places where the word *and* is used with names. Circle the word *and.* This is called a conjunction.

Grammar Guide
Conjunction - a word that joins words or sentences

b. When we see the conjunction *and* we know that two parts have been connected. What naming words were connected by the word *and* in **1a**?

____________________ ____________________

c. ________________ and ________________ play games on Saturday.
(*name of family member*) (*yourself*)

d. Make new sentences by using the conjunction *and.* Look at this example:
Bob went swimming. + Bill went swimming. = Bob and Bill went swimming.

Rewrite each of the two sentences as one sentence:

1) Sue can play. + Ann can play. = ____________________

2) Mom will cook dinner. + I will cook dinner. = ____________________

3) Dan went camping. + Jon went camping. = ____________________

4) Grandma can hug me. + Grandpa can hug me. = ____________________

5) Jack found a kitten. + I found a kitten. = ____________________

e. Spelling Bee

f. Enrichment

Read each list of words. Decide which category each word belongs in and copy that word under the correct heading.

Ex: cake soda cookie milk pie juice

Things you eat	Things you drink
cake cookie pie	soda juice milk

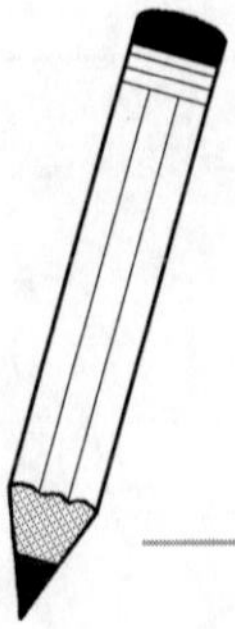

1) pencil notepad marker chalk paper blackboard

Things you write with	Things you write on

2) eagle hawk mouse rabbit weasel raven

Animals that fly	Animals that do not fly

3) rowboat ship car truck sailboat bike

Things that move on water	Things that move on land

Day 4 a. – b. Discussion with teacher.

c. When you have finished your letter look at the envelope below. Follow the format of the envelope in addressing your envelope.

stamp

Jacob Brown
10 Red Road
Anywhere, CA 90000

Hannah Jones
123 Fun Street
Somewhere, FL 30000

d. Mail your letter with your teacher's permission.

e. Spelling Pretest

f. Enrichment

Read each list of words. Decide which category each word belongs in and copy that word under the correct heading.

1) red square circle blue triangle green

Colors	Shapes

2) hop frog sit yell boy girl

Verbs, or doing words	Nouns, or naming words

3) airplane car truck helicopter rocket wagon

Things that move in the air	Things that move on land

Day 5 a. Read the directions at the end of this lesson. Follow them to make an easy paper airplane. With your teacher read the "Glossary of Words and Symbols" so you will know how to follow the directions. Remember to follow directions exactly so your airplane will fly!

Extra Activity: Make your own design for a paper airplane telling your teacher how to do each step along the way. When you are finished ask someone to try to make your airplane by following the directions you gave. Were they clear enough? Did you leave out any steps?

b. Spelling Test

c. Enrichment

Read each list of words. Decide which category each word belongs in and copy that word under the correct heading.

1) D 7 G 2 5 H

Letters	Numbers

2) cow horse calf foal bear cub

Baby animals	Adult animals

3) whale elephant spider butterfly giraffe worm

Big animals	Small animals

d. Journal Entry: Describe one of your favorite days.

e. Handwriting

Easy to Make Paper Airplane

Glossary of Words and Symbols

Shows the sides of the paper

Shows where the fold is to be made

Shows a crease made from a previous fold

Shows the direction the fold is to be made

<u>a, b, c, d, X's</u> — Letters are used to help in the direction

long ways — Fold to make the center fold down the longest part of the paper

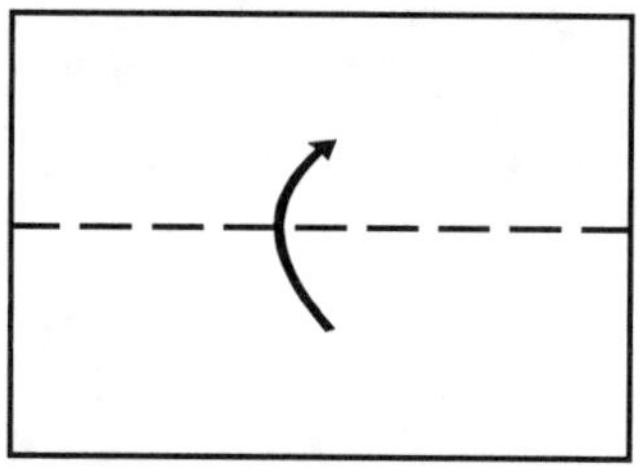

short ways — Fold to make the center fold down the shortest part of the paper

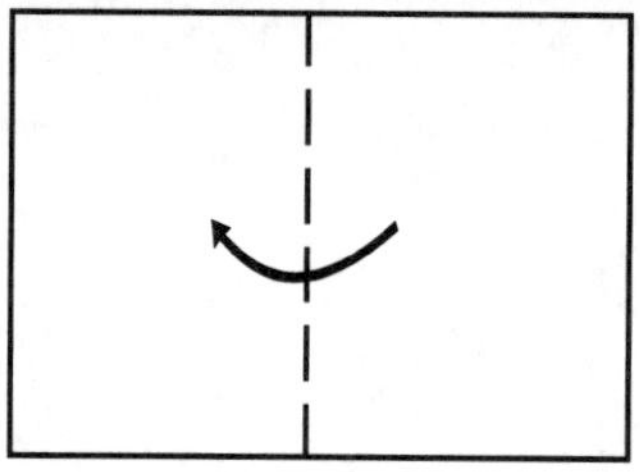

thumbcrease — To fold paper over with your thumb. The fold is the size of your thumb and used on back of wings.

notebook paper — Standard 3 hole notebook paper or plain copy or computer paper

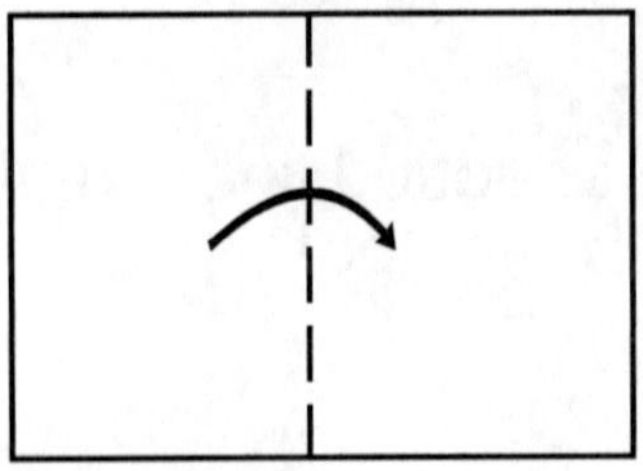

1. Fold paper in half short ways.
   Open paper.

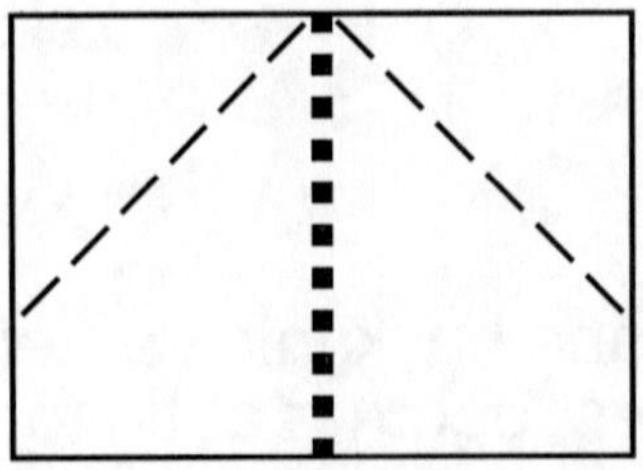

2. Fold corners to meet at the middle fold.

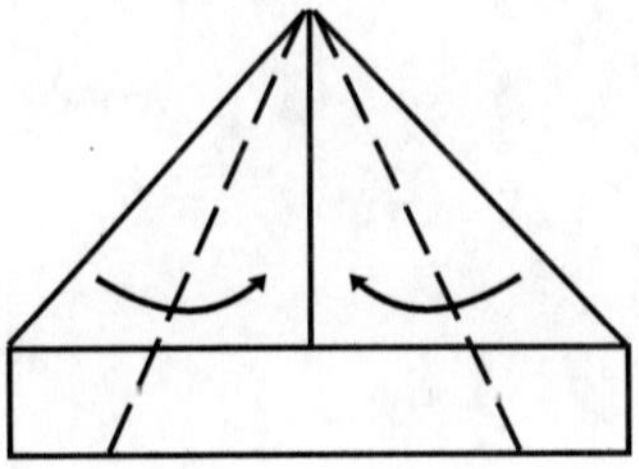

3. Fold sides over again to meet at middle fold (will overlap at bottom).

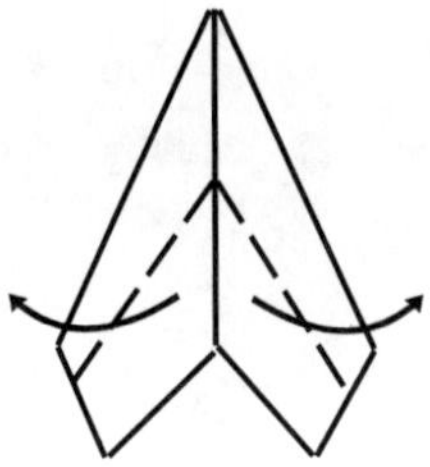

4. Fold wings back at dotted lines – wings overlap body at each side.

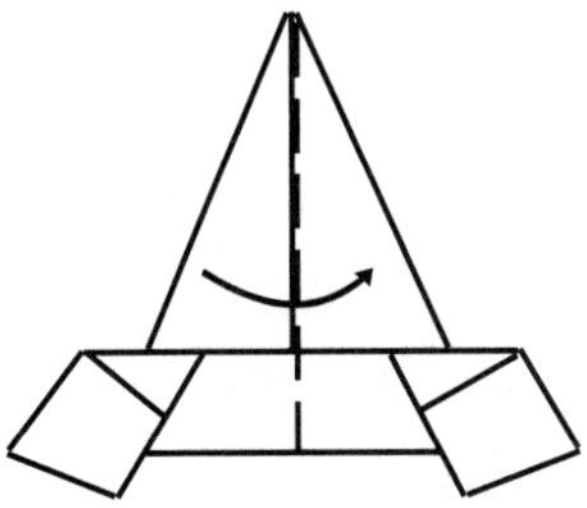

5. Fold plane in half – line up wings and crease fold.

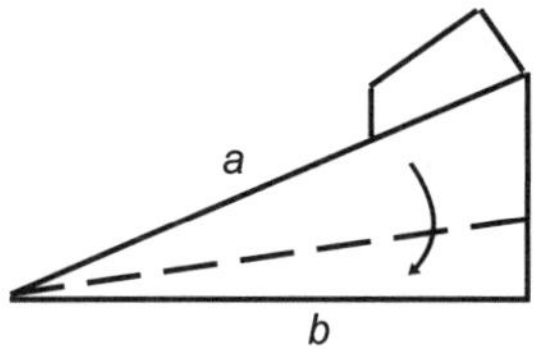

6. Fold down wing at dotted line – match side **a** with side **b** – on both sides.

7. Folding wing sides up.

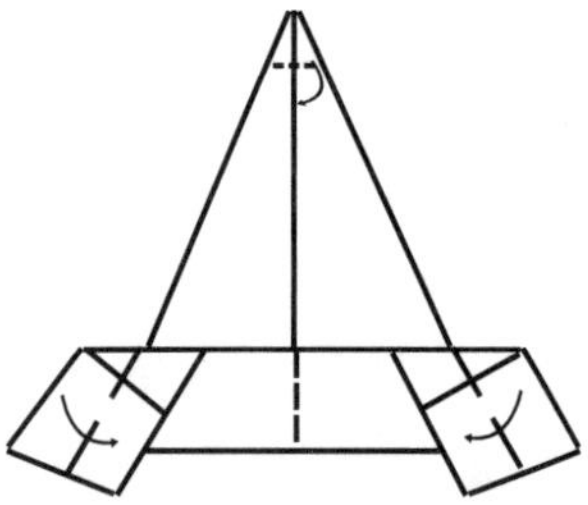

8. Fold nose of plane back into center fold. Press sides together at tip to hold it in place.

Flying Instruction:

Hold in middle of fuselage — holding the plane up a little bit, throw gently.

Review Activities

1. Label the parts of a friendly letter: signature greeting heading body closing

July 10, 2015

a. ____________________

Dear Abby,

b. ____________________

Hello. I hope you are having a fun vacation. I can hardly wait for you to come back.

c. ____________________

Love,

d. ____________________

Emma

e. ____________________

2. Rewrite the two sentences by using a conjunction to make one sentence.

a. Laura can run. Caleb can run.

____

b. Dad fixed the car. I fixed the car.

____

Assessment 2
(Lessons 7 – 9)

1. Write the contractions for these words.

   a. do not ____________________

   b. we are ____________________

   c. I will ____________________

   d. you will ____________________

   e. can not ____________________

   f. I am ____________________

2. Divide these words into syllables.

   a. riddle ____________________

   b. circle ____________________

   c. turtle ____________________

   d. summer ____________________

3. List these names in alphabetical order.

   Joe Dan Zack Mike ____________________

   ____

   ____

   ____

4. Rewrite the sentences by replacing the underlined words with synonyms.

a. This pillow is <u>soft</u>.

____

b. We like <u>big</u> dogs.

____

5. Rewrite the two sentences by using a conjunction to make one sentence.

a. Tom went fishing. Dan went fishing.

____

____

____

b. Lucy had fun. Emily had fun.

____

____

____

6. Write a proper noun for each common noun.

a. street ____________

b. city ____________

c. dog ____________

d. friend ____________

Notes

EVERYDAY WORDS

Raining, raining,
All night long;
Sometimes loud, sometimes soft,
Just like a song.

"Rain in the Night"
by Amelia Josephine Burr

Day 1 a. Write this poem from dictation, or copy it from the model. Compare your copy to the model and make corrections.

b.

Focus on Spelling

some somebody something sometimes somewhere

Bonus Word: night

Copy these spelling words. Say the words aloud as you write them.

c. Enrichment

Unscramble these letters to make your spelling words.

1) meingthso ______________________

2) bdyoomes ______________________

3) reheoemsw ______________________

4) mmeessoti ______________________

5) meos ______________________

Day 2 a. Discussion with teacher.

Grammar Guide
Verb - a doing word

b. Circle the suffix in this word: raining.

c. Discussion with teacher.

d. Add the suffix **-ing** to these doing words, or verbs, and act them out for others to guess:

1) laugh + ing ______________________

2) grow + ing ______________________

3) hold + ing ______________________

4) fall + ing ______________________

5) drink + ing ______________________

6) clean + ing ______________________

e. Use the words you made in **2d** to fill in the following blanks:

1) We are ______________________ the house.

2) The flowers in the garden are ______________________.

3) My mother is ______________________ the baby.

4) I was ______________________ at the clowns.

5) The bird was ______________________ from the bird bath.

6) The rain has been ______________________ all day.

f. **SEE-SPELL-SAY:** Look and **see** each word on the spelling list. **Spell** each word aloud. **Say** the word.

Day 3 a. Find two words in the poem that are opposites, or antonyms, and underline them with a red pencil or crayon.

Grammar Guide
Antonym - a word of opposite meaning

b. Look at the poem as your teacher reads these words. Find the antonym in the poem for each word she reads:

1) always ______________ 3) short ______________

2) day ______________ 4) none ______________

c. Read each sentence, and choose an opposite word that needs to be used in place of the italicized word:

bright small loud sweet long

1) The ringing alarm was *quiet*. ______________________

____

2) The ant is a very *big* bug. ______________________

____

3) The sugar is very *sour*. ______________________

____

4) The sun is very *dark* during the day. ______________

____

5) The *short* snake was lying across the road. __________

____

d. Discussion with teacher.

e. Spelling Bee

f. Enrichment

Read each list of words. Decide which category each word belongs in and copy that word under the correct heading.

1) Tuesday January Monday Saturday March December

Days of the week	Months of the year
______________	______________
______________	______________
______________	______________

2) boy James Sara girl friend Jack

Words that begin with a small letter	Words that begin with a capital letter
______________	______________
______________	______________
______________	______________

3) jump run man dog tree grow

<u>Verbs</u>	<u>Nouns</u>
______	______
______	______
______	______

Day 4 a. There are several words in our verse that end with the consonant pair **-ng**. Find and circle each one.

Phonics Fact

The vowel before **-ng** usually says its short sound.

b. Underline the **-ng** ending in each word.

long	king	rang
song	string	sang
strong	bring	bang
along	thing	clang

c. What vowel sound do the vowels make that come right before the letter **-ng**? Read the lists of words in **4b** to your teacher.

d. Choose words from the list in **4b** to fill in the blanks to rhyme with the underlined words.

1) The kite we will <u>bring</u> is on the end of a ______.

2) We heard the bell <u>clang</u> when the fire alarm ______.

3) When you learn the <u>song</u> we can all sing ______.

4) The golden, shiny <u>thing</u> sits on the head of a ______.

5) The rope holding the boat was <u>long</u>, and it was also ____________

6) We listened as the birds <u>sang</u>, and then we heard a gun go

____________.

e. Spelling Pretest

____________ ____________

____________ ____________

____________ ____________

f. Enrichment

Read the pair of words. How are they related? Write A, B, or C.

A – means the opposite
B – means almost the same
C – naming word and matching doing word

Ex: up : down – A (means the opposite)

1) big : little ____________

2) night : day ____________

3) lion : roar ____________

4) dog : bark ____________

5) cow : moo ____________

6) begin : start ____________

7) small : tiny ____________

8) pig : oink ____________

9) shy : timid ____________

10) over : above ____________

Day 5 a. Discussion with teacher.

b. Talk with your teacher about these expressions. Try to tell your teacher, or show her by acting or drawing, what you think these expressions mean:

1) She is feeling very sunny.
2) His face looks stormy.
3) That student is like a whirlwind.

c. Write a paragraph of three sentences telling what you see, hear, and feel when it rains. Begin your paragraph by indenting the first sentence. Write a fourth sentence telling what you think about rain. Remember to begin your sentences with a capital letter and end with a period.

d. On a separate piece of paper draw a picture describing your sentences. If you don't want to draw try to find pictures in a magazine that show rain. Save your picture.

e. Spelling Test

f. Journal Entry: Complete this thought: On rainy days I like...

g. Handwriting

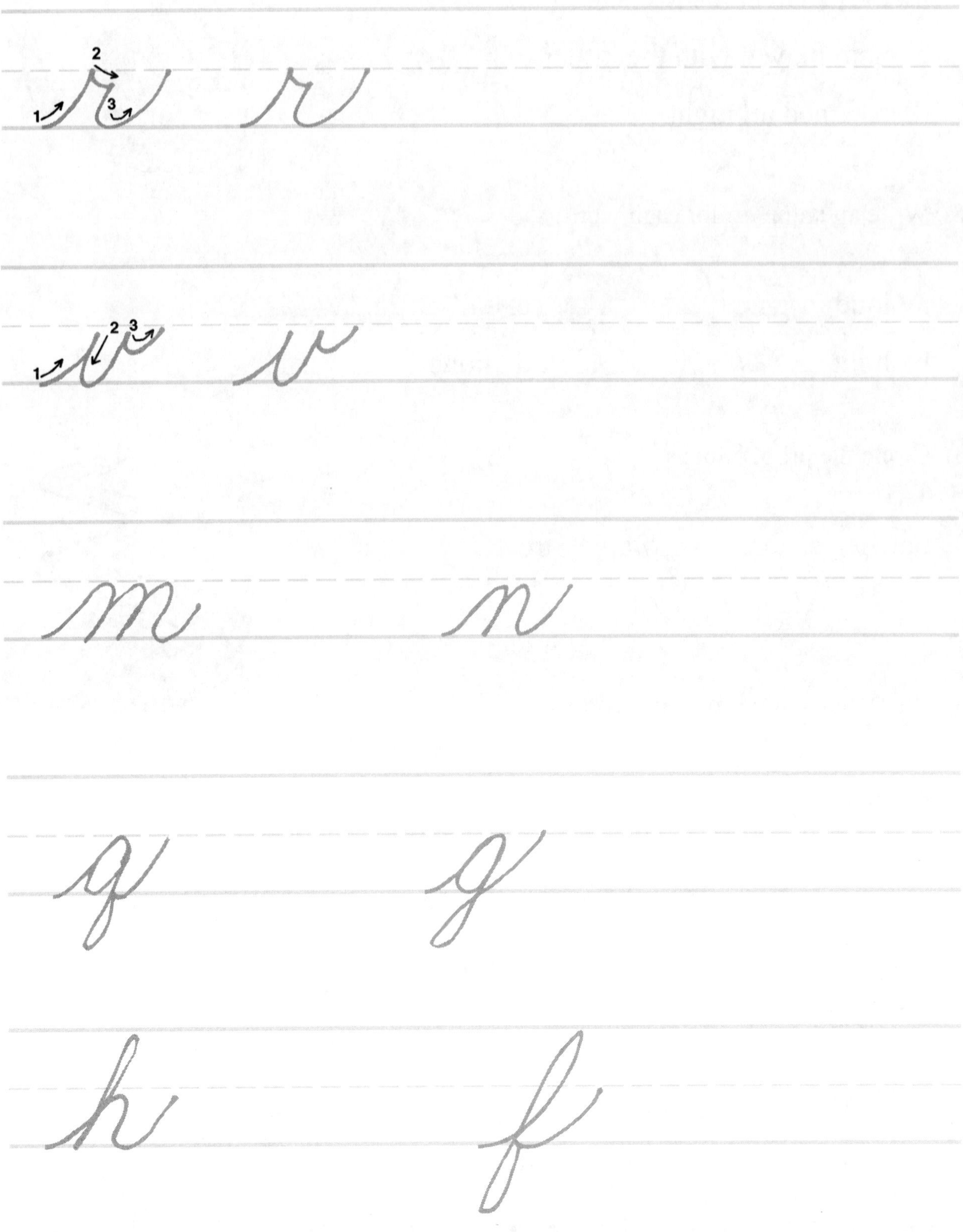

Review Activities

1. Circle the verb in each sentence.

a. Our plants grow every day.

b. I laughed at his jokes.

c. Sam played with the kitten.

d. It rained all night.

2. Write an antonym for each word.

a. loud ________________ c. tall ________________

b. light ________________ d. none ________________

3. Circle the proper nouns.

horse	sister	Maple Street
road	Maggie	Abi

4. Write a synonym for each word.

a. huge ________________

b. small ________________

c. run ________________

5. Add **-ing** to these doing words, or verbs.

a. jump________________ c. row ________________

b. crash ________________ d. fix ________________

There'll be rivers in the gutters
And lakes along the street.
It will make our lazy kitty
Wash his little, dirty feet.

"Rain in the Night"
by Amelia Josephine Burr

Day 1 a. Write the poem from dictation, or copy it from the model. Compare your copy to the model and make corrections.

b.

Focus on Spelling

dirty third girl bird first

Bonus Word: along

Copy these spelling words. Say the words aloud as you write them.

c. Enrichment

Fill in the blanks with letters to make your spelling words.

1) ☐ i r ☐

2) ☐ i r ☐

3) ☐ i r ☐ ☐

4) ☐ i r ☐ ☐

5) ☐ ☐ i r ☐

Day 2 a. Underline in red the word that tells about or describes the noun *kitty*.

Grammar Guide
Adjective - a word that describes a person, place, thing, or idea

b. Our sentence says that the kitty is *lazy*. *Lazy* is an adjective which describes the kitty. With a blue pencil underline the words that tell about the kitty's feet.

c. Using the three adjectives from our poem (*lazy, little, dirty*) think of nouns you can describe with these words. Remember, a noun names a person, place, thing, or idea. Make a list of at least two nouns that can go with each adjective:

1) lazy ____________ 2) little ____________ 3) dirty ____________

lazy ____________ little ____________ dirty____________

d. Read the following phrases to your teacher. Point out the adjective in each phrase:

1) a slow boat	3) a soft pillow	5) a rainy day
2) the sleepy dog	4) the big house	6) the happy baby

e. Can you imagine what this kitty looks like and acts like? Describe, draw, or act out what you think this kitty might be like.

f. **SEE-SPELL-SAY:** Look and **see** each word on the spelling list. **Spell** each word aloud. **Say** the word.

Day 3 a. Circle the words in your sentences that have two of the same consonant letters in the middle.

Phonics Fact

Syllable - part of a word which has a single vowel sound

b. Clap and say each of these words. How many syllables do you hear in each word?

1) summer______	4) little______	7) happy______
2) hello______	5) dinner______	8) better______
3) middle______	6) gutter______	9) bigger______

c. Divide the words you read in **3a** by drawing a line between the two consonant letters that are the same.

gutters kitty little

d. Spelling Bee

e. Enrichment

Read the pair of words. How are they related? Write A, B, or C.

A – means the opposite
B – means almost the same
C – naming word and matching doing word

1) end : finish ______
2) top : bottom ______
3) bird : fly______
4) close : shut ______
5) clean : dirty______
6) dry : wet ______
7) run : jog ______
8) hot : cold ______
9) horse : trots ______
10) monkey : climbs ______

Day 4 a. Read the following clues. Write the correct word in each blank. The answers are found in the literature passage:

1) I want to learn to ____________. (Lesson 7)
2) ... he knew that she was ____________ for Carol. (Lesson 4)
3) Dear Grandma and ____________, (Lesson 9)
4) Raining, ____________, All night long; (Lesson 10)
5) Can people ____________ whistles? (Lesson 8)
6) There'll be ____________ in the gutters. (Lesson 11)
7) Peter was sitting by ____________. (Lesson 2)

b. Use the words you found in **4a** to complete this crossword puzzle. The number at the beginning of each row tells you which word goes in each row. (The rows can go from top to bottom or from side to side.) A shaded box means that two words will share a letter, so don't write the letter twice. Remember to write one letter in each box.

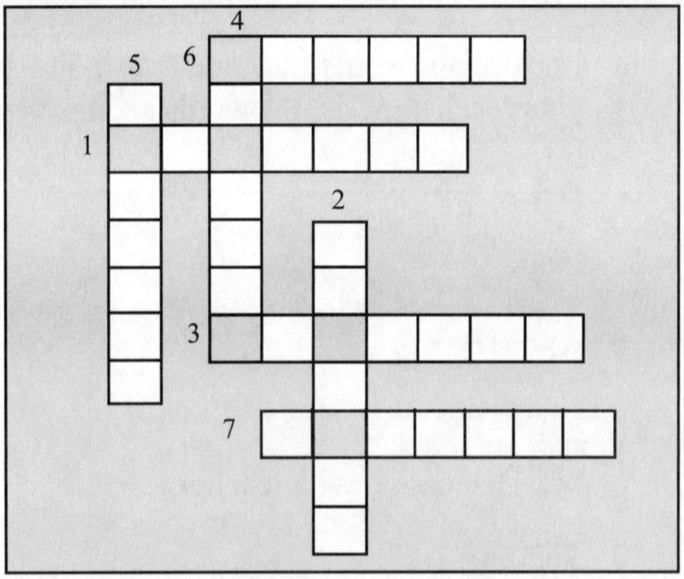

Across
1) Answer from #1
3) Answer from #3
6) Answer from #6
7) Answer from #7

Down
2) Answer from #2
4) Answer from #4
5) Answer from #5

c. Spelling Pretest

______________________ ______________________

______________________ ______________________

______________________ ______________________

d. Enrichment

Read the pair of words. How are they related? Write A, B, or C.

A – means the opposite
B – means almost the same
C – naming word and matching doing word

1) quiet : silent ________

2) chop : cut ________

3) carpenter : builds ________

4) cool : warm ________

5) fall : rise ________

6) exit : enter ________

7) clever : smart ________

8) cat : meows ________

9) duck : quacks ________

10) together : apart ________

Day 5 a. Look up the words *river* and *lake* in the dictionary. Discuss the meanings with your teacher. Write the words and their meanings as you understand them.

____

____

____

____

b. – c. Discussion with teacher.

d. Spelling Test

______________ ______________

______________ ______________

______________ ______________

e. Enrichment

Read the pair of words. How are they related? Write A, B, or C.

A – means the opposite
B – means almost the same
C – naming word and matching doing word

1) thin : slender ________

2) tall : short ________

3) horn : beeps ________

4) girl : cooks ________

5) stiff : hard ________

6) baby : sleeps ________

7) rabbit : hops ________

8) bright : colorful ________

9) dark : light ________

10) strong : weak ________

f. Journal Entry: What water activities do you enjoy? Make a list of them. Write a few sentences about one.

g. Handwriting

Review Activities

1. Circle the adjectives in the phrases.

   a. the lazy dog
   b. the little child
   c. the dirty cat
   d. the soft bed

2. Divide the words into syllables.

   a. happy ____________ c. middle ____________
   b. dinner ____________ d. puddle ____________

3. In each sentence underline the nouns and circle the verb.

   a. Ryan ran to the park.
   b. Sarah ate all of her dinner.
   c. Her horse jumped high over the fence.
   d. My dog loves bones.

4. Rewrite each sentence and replace the underlined word with an antonym.

   a. The oak tree is <u>short</u>. ____________________

   ____

   b. Mike likes his <u>old</u> bicycle. ____________________

   ____

   c. We ate dinner <u>late</u>. ____________________

   ____

The roses will wear diamonds
Like kings and queens at court;
But the pansies all get muddy
Because they are so short.

"Rain in the Night"
by Amelia Josephine Burr

Day 1 a. Write this poem from dictation, or copy it from the model. Compare your copy to the model and make corrections.

b.

Focus on Spelling

wear year clear hear dear

Bonus Word: queen

Copy these spelling words. Say the words aloud as you write them.

c. Enrichment

Find your spelling words in this puzzle.

Find the word puzzle for : wear year clear hear dear

w	d	f	r	o	m	b
i	e	w	e	a	r	y
t	a	l	e	a	t	e
h	r	w	f	r	o	a
b	h	e	a	r	d	r
y	c	l	e	a	r	g

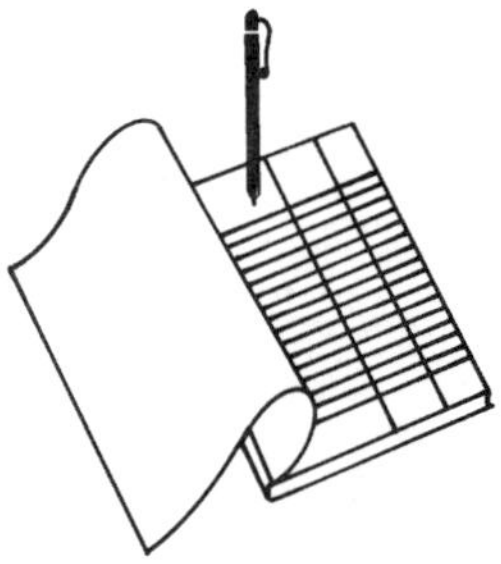

Day 2 a. Underline each of the nouns, or naming words, that name more than one.

b. How did we make each naming word mean more than one? What letter did we add to the end?

c. The word *pansies* is a little different. One of these flowers is called a *pansy*. This is the singular form, meaning single or one. When you make a word mean more than one, it is called plural.

Grammar Guide
Singular - one **Plural** - more than one

Look at this word, and tell how we changed it to mean more than one or plural: pansy – pansies

Grammar Guide
If a word ends with a consonant and y, change the **y** to **i** and add **es**.

d. Change these words to mean more than one:

1) body ________ 3) pony ________ 5) copy ________

2) baby ________ 4) candy ________ 6) jelly ________

e. **SEE-SPELL-SAY:** Look and **see** each word on the spelling list. **Spell** each word aloud. **Say** the word.

Day 3

a. Find the word in our poem that has double consonant letters in the middle of the word. Underline the word, and then draw a line to divide this word into two syllables.

b. As you learned in Lesson 11, when there are double consonant letters in the middle of the word, you divide the word into syllables between the middle consonants.
Ex: bet/ter

Divide these words into syllables:

1) slipper
2) runner
3) batter
4) swimmer
5) happen
6) letter

c. As you learned in Lesson 7, when a word ends with a consonant and **-le**, you usually divide the word before the consonant which comes before **-le**.
Ex: whis/tle

Divide these words into syllables:

1) handle
2) rustle
3) beetle
4) trouble
5) circle
6) cradle

d. Spelling Bee

e. Enrichment

Read the pair of words. How are they related? Write A, B, or C.

A – means the opposite
B – means almost the same
C – naming word and matching doing word

1) hen : clucks ________
2) rooster : crows ________
3) funny : humorous ________
4) fix : mend ________
5) loud : noisy________
6) fast : slow ________
7) boys : play ________
8) center : middle ________
9) grin : smile ________
10) breezy : windy ________

Day 4 a. Discussion with teacher.

Using Your Tools

The **encyclopedia** is a book or set of books that contains information on various topics.

b. Look up the names of the following flowers in an encyclopedia or a book about flowers so you can see what they look like:

tulip
rose
pansy
sunflower
daisy

c. Write sentences describing each flower. Remember to use many describing words (adjectives) to tell about the color, size, and shape of each flower.

d. On a separate piece of paper you may draw pictures of these flowers or cut them out of magazines or seed catalogs.

e. Spelling Pretest

________________ ________________

________________ ________________

________________ ________________

f. Enrichment

Read the pair of words. How are they related? Write A, B, or C.

A – means the opposite
B – means almost the same
C – naming word and matching doing word

1) fold : bend ________

2) under : beneath ________

3) narrow : thin ________

4) yell : whisper ________

5) sweet : sour ________

6) fish : swims ________

7) dolphin : leaps ________

8) garbage : trash ________

9) tricky : cunning ________

10) snake : slithers ________

Day 5 a. Find the simile in our poem and read it to your teacher.

Focus on Writing

A **simile** compares two things by using the words **like** or **as.**

Ex: hungry ***as*** a lion
swims ***like*** a fish

b. Read these similes, and try to imagine how they might look:
clouds that look like cotton balls
raindrops that shine like jewels
a kite that flies like a bird
flowers that smell like perfume

You may want to draw pictures that go with these similes on a separate piece of paper.

c. Try to think of words to complete the following similes:

1) The boys were jumping around like ______________________.

2) The blanket was soft like ______________________.

3) The water was blue like ______________________.

4) The light was bright like ______________________.

d. Write three to four similes on your own. You may look back at your description in **4c** and compare the flowers.

e. Practice the first and second verses of the poem. Memorize verse three.

f. Spelling Test

g. Enrichment

Read the pair of words. How are they related? Write A, B, or C.

A – means the opposite
B – means almost the same
C – naming word and matching doing word

1) student : learns ______

2) teacher : teaches ______

3) ill : sick ______

4) near : far ______

5) shiny : dull ______

6) look : see ______

7) summer : winter ______

8) hot : cold ______

9) wild : tame ______

10) bride : groom ______

h. Journal Entry: Choose a tree or bush in your yard.
Describe it in detail.

i. Handwriting

Review Activities

1. Write the plural, or the word which means more than one.

a. baby ____________________

b. jelly ____________________

c. pansy ____________________

d. copy ____________________

2. Divide the words into syllables.

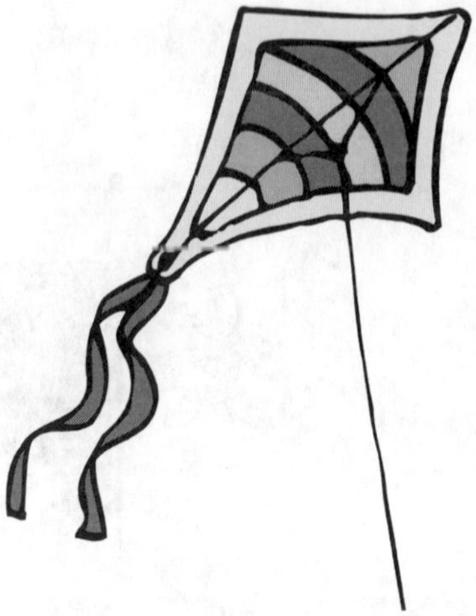

a. bubble ____________________

b. trouble ____________________

c. swimmer ____________________

d. happen ____________________

3. Complete these sentences to make a simile.

a. The kite rose high like ______________________________.

b. The flower was pretty like ______________________________.

4. Write a contraction for each pair of words.

a. do not ____________________

b. I will ____________________

c. is not ____________________

d. are not ____________________

I'll sail my boat tomorrow
In wonderful new places,
But first I'll take my watering pot
And wash the pansies' faces.

"Rain in the Night"
by Amelia Josephine Burr

Day 1 a. Write this poem from dictation, or copy it. Compare your copy to the model and make corrections.

b.

Focus on Spelling

sail wait plain raise hair

Bonus Word: tomorrow

Copy these spelling words. Say the words aloud as you write them.

c. Enrichment

Fill in the blanks to make your spelling words.

1) _ _ a i _

2) _ a i _

3) 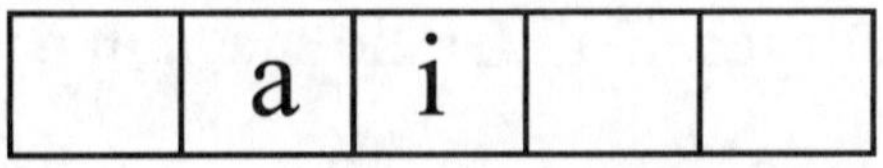

4) 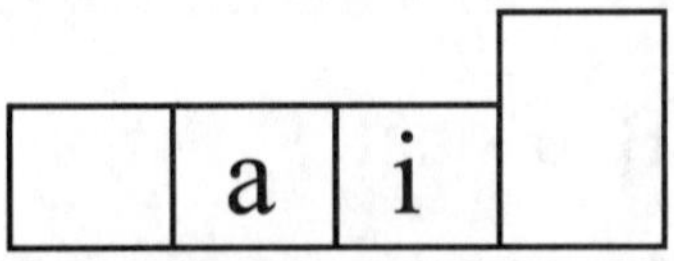

5) 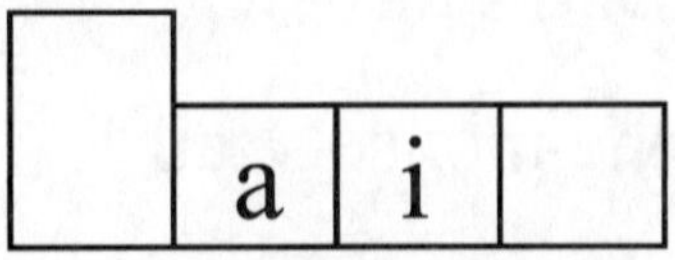

d. Review the spelling words from lessons 10 – 12

Day 2 a. – b. Discussion with teacher.

c. Do the same with the words *wonderful* and *watering*. Listen as your teacher says them, then say and clap the words. Divide the words into syllables by drawing lines between the syllables.

wonderful watering

d. Divide these three syllable words. Here is an example: re/mem/ber

1) yesterday 2) afternoon 3) beginning 4) covering

e. **SEE-SPELL-SAY:** Look and **see** each word on the spelling list. **Spell** each word aloud. **Say** the word.

Day 3 a. The apostrophe is a mark that looks like this: (’). Circle each word in the poem with an apostrophe.

b.

Punctuation Pointer

Apostrophe - Use an apostrophe **s** (**’s**) to show that something belongs to something or someone.

Grammar Guide

Singular possessive noun - a singular noun with an apostrophe **s** (**’s**) to show that something belongs to something or someone

Look at these phrases with your teacher. Circle the **'s** in each phrase.

1) the dog's dish
2) Mother's coat
3) the boy's bike
4) Ann's doll
5) the cat's claws
6) Bob's hat
7) Dad's tie
8) the mouse's tail

c. Orally or in writing answer each question using the phrases above:

1) What belongs to the dog? ______
2) What belongs to Mother? ______
3) What belongs to the boy? ______
4) What belongs to Ann? ______
5) What belongs to the cat? ______
6) What belongs to Bob? ______
7) What belongs to Dad? ______
8) What belongs to the mouse? ______

d. Make up three phrases telling about things that belong to you. Use your name, add **'s**, and then tell the name of something that belongs to you. Ex: Bill's bike

1)______
2)______
3)______

e. In this week's poem the word *pansies'* has an apostrophe to tell us that something belongs to the pansies. What belongs to them?

______

Grammar Guide

Plural possessive noun - a plural noun with an apostrophe (') to show that something belongs to something or someone

f. We put an apostrophe after a plural word that ends with **s** to show that something belongs to that naming word, or noun. This is called a plural possessive noun.
Ex: collars belonging to dogs – dogs' collars

Write the correct way to show these things:

1) hats belonging to ladies ______________________

2) hands belonging to clocks ______________________

3) toys belonging to sisters ______________________

4) houses belonging to friends ______________________

g. Spelling Bee

Day 4 a. Review the work you did in Lesson 11 on adjectives.

b. Underline the two adjectives that describe the places where the boat will sail.

Think of at least two adjectives to describe the boat. ______________________

____

c. Find the word cards for Lesson 13 on page 381. Cut them out. Mix up each group of cards and place the nouns face down on one side and the adjectives face down on the other. Take turns turning over one noun and one adjective. If the two words go together, you get another turn.

d. Choose two of the noun/adjective pairs. Write a complete sentence with each pair.

e. Spelling Pretest

f. Enrichment

Read the pair of words. How are they related? Write A, B, or C.

A – means the opposite
B – means almost the same
C – naming word and matching doing word

1) high : low ________
2) always : never ________
3) glad : happy ________
4) eagle : soars ________
5) squirrel : chatters ________
6) weary : tired ________
7) north : south ________
8) rich : wealthy________
9) deer : prances ________
10) east : west ________

Day 5. a. – b. Discussion with teacher.

c. Spelling Test

______________________ ______________________

______________________ ______________________

______________________ ______________________

d. Enrichment

Read the pair of words. How are they related? Write A, B, or C.

A – whole : part
B – in a sequence
C – naming word and matching doing word

1) pig : snout ________
2) cat : claw ________
3) eyes : see ________
4) tailor : sews ________
5) oven : bakes ________
6) hammer : pounds ________
7) first : second ________
8) more : most ________
9) January : February ________
10) monkey : tail ________

e. Journal Entry: What places would you like to visit? Make a list. Find each one on a map.

f. Handwriting

Review Activities

1. Divide these words into syllables.

   a. yesterday ____________________

   b. covering ____________________

2. Write the possessive form using an apostrophe.
   Ex: the dish belongs to the dog <u>the dog's dish</u>

   a. the hat belongs to Mom ________________________________

   b. the car belongs to Tom ________________________________

   c. the bike belongs to the boy ________________________________

3. Write the plural possessive form using an apostrophe.
   Ex: the dishes belong to the dogs <u>the dogs' dishes</u>

   a. the toys belong to the friends ________________________________

   b. the cars belong to the brothers ________________________________

   c. the flowers belong to the ladies ________________________________

4. In each sentence fill in the blank with an adjective that describes the noun.

   a. Look at the ____________________ building.

   b. Did you see that ____________________ car?

   c. Mom wants a ____________________ flower.

   d. We saw a ____________________ bird at the park.

Assessment 3
(Lessons 10 – 13)

1. Circle the verb, or doing word, in these sentences.

   a. That tree grew tall.

   b. The boy ran quickly.

   c. I hop on one foot.

2. Write an antonym, or a word of opposite meaning, for these words.

   a. bright ____________

   b. little ____________

   c. always ____________

3. Circle the adjectives, or describing words.

   a. the loud noise

   b. the silly boy

   c. the happy mom

4. Divide these words into syllables.

   a. middle ____________

   b. trouble ____________

   c. funnel ____________

   d. tomorrow ____________

   e. circle ____________

   f. yesterday ____________

5. Write the plural, or the word that means more than one.

   a. baby ____________________

   b. lady ____________________

   c. jelly ____________________

6. Write the possessive noun.

   a. the book belongs to Joe ____________________

   b. the boat belongs to the man ____________________

7. Write the plural possessive noun.

   a. the cars belong to the boys ____________________

   b. the dog belong to the sisters ____________________

Notes

LITERATURE LINK

Day 1 Listen to your teacher read the French vocabulary words.

French Vocabulary

jeune fille (zhun fee) – *girl*
famille (fa – mee) – *family*
frere (rhymes with "where") – *brother*
metro (me-tro) – *subway*
maison (may-zon) – *house*
Bois de Bologne (Bwa de Bu-lon-ya) – *Woods of Bologne*
velos (ve-lo rhymes with "hello") – *bicycle*
Tour de France (Tour rhymes with "poor") – *a yearly race*
la glace (la-glas) – *ice cream*
au chocolat (oh shock-o-lat) – *chocolate*
la glace a la fraise (a la frays) – *strawberry ice cream*
merci (mare-see) – *thank you*
au revoir (oh re-vwa) – *goodbye*
allo (ah-low) – *hello*

Discussion with your teacher.

Begin reading the story, "A Jeune Fille Named Marie." You will have time tomorrow to finish the story.

A Jeune Fille Named Marie

Marie lives in a city called Paris. Paris is the biggest city in France. Marie and her **famille** ("fa-mee" – family) like to visit all the wonderful places in town. She goes with her mother, father and **frere** (rhymes with "where" – brother). His name is Pierre. Marie and Pierre like to ride the bus and the **metro**.

Pierre plays **football** (soccer), and Marie loves to dance. They go from their **maison** ("may-zon" – house) to the park to play. Their favorite park is the **Bois de Bologne** ("Bwa de Bu-lon-ya" – woods of Bologne). Many of the parks and gardens in Paris were built for the kings and queens of France only. Now all the people of Paris may enjoy these parks.

At the park Marie and Pierre also get to ride their **velos** ("velo" – bicycle). Many people in France like to ride their velos. A race is held every year called the **Tour de France** (Tour rhymes with "poor" – a yearly race). People all over the world watch this race on T.V. It takes a long time to finish. The winner is a big star in France.

After they play Marie and Pierre like to have a snack. Mother brings them **la glace** ("la glace" – ice cream). Pierre likes **la glace au chocolat** best. Marie likes **la glace a la fraise** ("a la frays" – strawberry ice cream) best. Pierre and Marie tell mother **merci** ("mare-see" – thank you) for the snack. Then it is time to go home. It has been a fun and busy day.

As Marie, Pierre, Father, and Mother go back home, it is time to say **au revoir** ("oh re-vwa" – good bye). If you go to France you can use some of the new words you learned. If you ever meet someone from France be sure to say **allo**! ("ah-low" – hello)

Day 2 a. Finish reading the book or story from yesterday

b. **Discussion Questions for *Madeline*:**

1) Where does Madeline live?
2) Who does Madeline live with?
3) What problem did Madeline have?
4) Who came to visit Madeline?
5) What was the surprise Madeline showed her friends?
6) What was Miss Clavel's next problem?
7) Why did the little girls want to have an operation?
8) What did Miss Clavel say to the little girls when they cried?

Discussion Questions for "A Jeune Fille Named Marie":

1) Who is this story about? Name the four people in the story.
2) What city do Pierre and Marie live in? What country do they live in? What city and country do you live in?

3) How do Pierre and Marie travel around in Paris? How do you travel around the place you live?
4) What is Pierre's favorite sport? What does Marie like to do? What do you like to do for fun?
5) Pierre and Marie went to a park with their parents. Who were the parks first built for?
6) What do Marie and Pierre like to ride? Do you like to ride your bike? What is the famous race for cyclists in France called?
7) Snacks are good after you play. What is Pierre's favorite snack? What is Marie's favorite snack? What is your favorite snack?
8) What would you say to someone you meet who speaks French? What would you say when he leaves?

c. Here is a map of Paris.

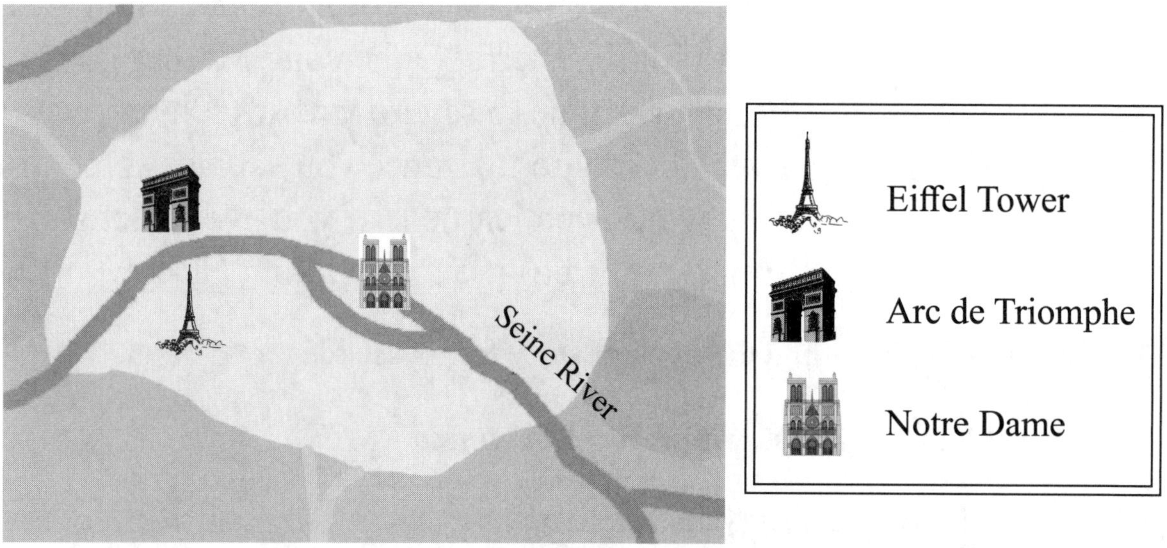

Locate the following places on your map:

1) Eiffel Tower
2) Cathedral of Notre Dame (No-tru Dam)
3) Arc de Triomphe (Ark de Tree-omphe)

d. These are all famous places in Paris. Look up these three sites in an encyclopedia (see France or Paris) or the Internet, or read the information given. Write the names under the correct pictures.

Eiffel Tower - Built for the World's Fair in 1889, this tower is now the symbol for Paris. It is 984 feet high.

The Cathedral of Notre Dame – This cathedral (church) was finished in the year 1263. It is located on an island in the center of Paris, called the Isle de la Cite (Eel-de-la-See-Tay). The stained glass windows of this cathedral are beautiful with its rose windows being world famous. Victor Hugo's novel *The Hunchback of Notre Dame* was written about this place.

Arc de Triomphe – The Arch of Triumph, as it is known, is located at the Place de l'Etoile (the Place of the Star). Twelve avenues come together at the Place de l'Etoile (plas-de-le-twah) forming a star shape. The Arch of Triumph is the largest and most well-known stone arch in the world. It was begun by the Emperor Napoleon in 1806 as a monument to his victories. It was completed in 1836 and dedicated to "All French armies since 1792." The burial place of France's Unknown Soldier is there.

e. After listening to your teacher read the information, or after reading it yourself, tell the importance of each site.

f. Locate the following places in Ludwig Bemelman's book, *Madeline:*
   1) The Opera
   2) Place Vendome
   3) The Cathedral of Notre Dame
   4) The Basilica of Sacre-Coeur
   5) Eiffel Tower

Day 3 a. Many children live in countries other than America. Talk with your teacher about things that may be the same with children in other countries. This is called comparing. Talk with your teacher about things that may be different. This is called contrasting.

Discuss these things that are similar for all children.

1) Families
2) Need for food and clothing
3) School or learning
4) Play

b. While all children have things in common there are also many things that are different. Talk with your teacher about the ways life may be different for children in countries other than America:

1) Language
2) Customs
3) Religion
4) Need to work
5) Opportunities for the future

c. Using magazines or catalogs, find pictures of children from different countries. Get a piece of construction or drawing paper, and glue these pictures on it. This is called a collage. Try to find as many different aged children as you can.

d. On the back of your collage make two headings like this:

Same **Different**

Now make a list of the ways you are the same as the children in your collage and ways that you are different. Include at least four items on each list.

e. Optional: You may want to pick a foreign country and find out what life is like for a child in that country. Ask your teacher for help in finding reference material.

Day 4 a. Find each of the words in the box in the Word Search. Circle the word in the box after you have found it in the Word Search. Remember words can go top to bottom or side to side.

Ex: The word *big* is inside this Word Search going from top to bottom. *Dog* is going from left to right. Words can share letters. *Big* and *dog* share the letter **g**.

W	U	B	N
X	R	I	S
D	O	G	Y

Look at the first few letters of your word to try to find it. Ask your teacher for help if you have trouble completing this activity.

b. Find these words from our story, "A Jeune Fille Named Marie":

Word Search I

frere	Paris	famille
favorite	Marie	maison

F	S	O	P	A	R	I	S	L
R	M	R	T	L	G	F	B	F
E	A	F	A	R	I	L	B	A
R	M	A	I	S	O	N	T	V
E	N	M	Q	U	K	D	F	O
B	F	I	B	Y	R	S	H	R
L	G	L	C	X	U	A	V	I
P	K	L	A	J	P	O	B	T
O	H	E	X	M	A	R	I	E

Word Search II

Pierre	France	metro
velo	glace	allo

S	J	C	O	W	E	M	C	M
C	M	E	T	R	O	R	T	G
W	U	T	N	T	B	P	L	L
P	L	O	D	N	M	I	J	A
K	L	S	J	M	F	E	G	C
A	L	L	O	M	D	R	E	E
I	J	G	N	S	M	R	I	T
N	F	R	A	N	C	E	C	N
C	N	S	Y	E	V	E	L	O

c. Tell your teacher what each of the French words mean.

1) frere ________________

2) famille ________________

3) maison ________________

4) velos ________________

5) metro ________________

6) la glace ________________

7) allo ________________

Day 5 a. You have been introduced to lists of spelling words in Lessons 7 – 13. Review these spelling words.

________________ ________________

________________ ________________

________________ ________________

________________ ________________

b. Take dictation from teacher.

____

____

c. Discussion with teacher.

____

____

I **C.A.N.** Assessment
Literature Link on *Paris*

After the Literature Link on *Paris* is completed check off each I **C.A.N.** objective with your teacher.

_____	**C**	I can **complete** my work.
_____		I can be **creative**.
_____	**A**	I can be **accurate**.
_____		I can do my work with a good **attitude**.
_____	**N**	I can do my work **neatly**.

Notes

EVERYDAY WORDS

A record 5.7 million people visited the Eiffel Tower, France's most popular tourist attraction, in 1990.

From *The Tampa Tribune,* Feb. 3, 1991

Day 1 a. Read the sentence along with your teacher. Copy it. Compare your copy to the model and make corrections.

b.

Focus on Spelling

who what when where why

Bonus Word: reporter

Copy these spelling words. Say the words aloud as you write them.

c. Enrichment

Find your spelling words in this puzzle: who what when where why

w	h	a	t	o	m	b
h	a	b	o	v	e	a
o	w	h	y	e	t	l
h	t	w	h	e	n	o
b	e	h	i	n	d	n
y	w	h	e	r	e	g

Day 2 a. Discussion with teacher.

> **Using Your Tools**
>
> The **newspaper** gives you current events, weather, sports, and much more.

b. Using the index of your local newspaper find the following sections.

1) Sports
2) World
3) Editorials
4) Comics
5) Classified Section

c. Discussion with teacher.

d. Choose two or three pictures you like from the newspaper. With your teacher read the caption (words telling about the picture). Try to think of your own description for each picture.

____

____

____

____

e. **SEE-SPELL-SAY:** Look and **see** each word on the spelling list. **Spell** each word aloud. **Say** the word.

Day 3 a. In the sentence from Day 1 there is a word that uses an apostrophe to show that something belongs to it. Underline that word.

b. What belongs to France? ____________________

c. Look at the three sets of sentences. Some of the italicized words need apostrophes, and some are just plural nouns. Which of the underlined words need an apostrophe added? Circle the word and add the apostrophe.

1) The *dogs* love to play with the ball.
Bring the *dogs* water dish into the house.

2) It is good to read a lot of *books*.
Look at that *books* cover.

3) I went with my mother to pick out my *fathers* new shirt.
Both of my roommates sent their *fathers* a present.

d. Spelling Bee

e. Enrichment

Read the pair of words. How are they related? Write A, B, or C.

A – whole : part
B – in a sequence
C – naming word and matching doing word

Ex. first : second B
flower : stem A

1) hand : finger ________
2) tree : grows ________
3) morning : afternoon ________
4) arm : elbow ________
5) fan : blows ________
6) day : night ________
7) bike : wheel ________
8) Monday : Tuesday ________
9) ears : hear ________
10) 7 : 8 ________

Day 4. a. Circle the word in our sentence with the letters **-tion**.

Phonics Fact
-tion says /**shun**/

b. Listen as your teacher reads this list of words. Underline the letters in each word that say /**shun**/. Also, after hearing the list of words read, draw lines dividing the words into syllables.

1) vacation	3) pollution	5) attraction
2) collection	4) station	6) caption

c. Orally make up sentences using each of the **-tion** words in **4b**. Tell your teacher what you think each word means. Using your dictionary look up any words you don't know.

d. Use the **-tion** words from **4b** to fill in the blanks in these sentences:

vacation	pollution	attraction
collection	station	caption

1) The river is not clean because of ______________.

2) We are going on a family ______________ to the beach.

3) Bob will add another baseball card to his ______________.

4) We must go to the gas ______________ to get gas for the car.

5) There is a ______________ under the picture telling what it is.

6) The best ______________ is the big ride at the fair.

e. Spelling Pretest

______________ ______________

______________ ______________

______________ ______________

f. Enrichment

Read the pair of words. How are they related? Write A, B, or C.

A – whole : part
B – in a sequence
C – naming word and matching doing word

1) foot : toe ______

2) bird : fly ______

3) first : second ______

4) head : ear ______

5) word : letter ______

6) fish : swim ______

7) tree : leaf ______

8) door : knob ______

9) 9 : 10 ______

10) book : page ______

Day 5 a. What facts, or true statements, do you see in our passage? Make a written list of the facts.

b. With your teacher choose a newspaper article to read. Use a highlighter pen to mark three facts, or true statements, that are in your news article.

c. After reading the article answer these questions about it:

1) **Who** is the article about? ______________________

____

2) **What** happened in the article? ______________________

____

3) **When** did the story take place? ______________________

____

4) **Where** did the story take place? ______________________

____

5) **Why** was the story written?

What did the person who wrote the story want people to know

____

____

d. Think of an event you know about such as a special family event, birthday party, or holiday celebration. Pretend you are a newspaper reporter and orally, or in writing, tell your teacher the answers to these questions:

1) **Who** attended the event?
2) **What** event was being celebrated?
3) **When** did the event take place?
4) **Where** did the event take place?
5) **Why** was the event held?

____

____

____

____

Optional: If you want to write a story about this event you may include pictures and captions.

e. Spelling Test

f. Journal Entry: Write about a favorite trip.

g. Handwriting

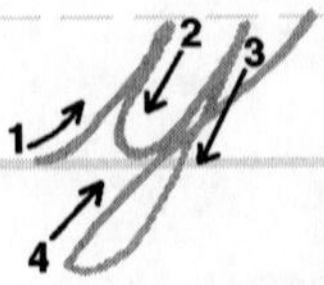 y

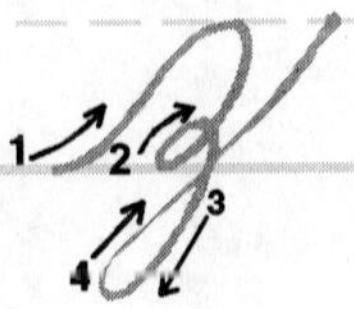 z

b k

p j

w x

Review Activities

1. Read the sentences and decide which word needs an apostrophe. Write the apostrophe.

   a. The *cats* love that ball.

      This is the *cats* ball.

   b. The *books* cover is torn.

      Tom has six *books*.

2. Read these sentences. List two facts.

   Science is the best subject. Today I learned that the sun is very big. It gives us heat and light. I am glad we have the sun.

   ____

   ____

   ____

   ____

3. Write the possessive form using an apostrophe.
   Ex: the toy belongs to the dog – <u>the dog's toy</u>

   a. the book belongs to Sarah ____________________

   b. The shirt belongs to Dad ____________________

   c. the bike belongs to the girl ____________________

4. Write the plural possessive form using an apostrophe.
   Ex: the dishes belong to the dogs – <u>the dogs' dishes</u>

   a. the blocks belong to the boys ____________________

   b. the dresses belong to the girls ____________________

   c. the clocks belong to the ladies ____________________

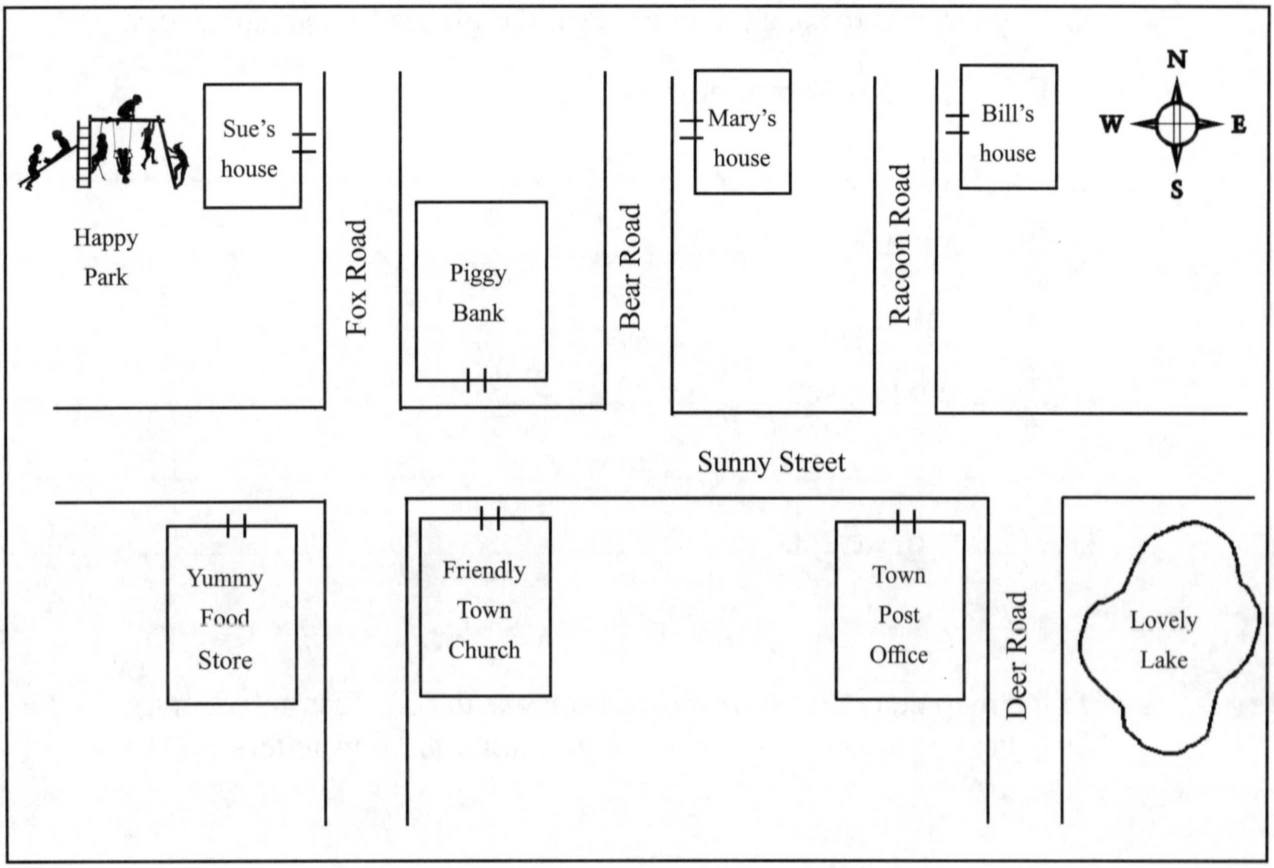

Day 1 a. Here is a simple map of Friendly Town. On our map you can find streets, buildings, a lake, and a park.

Using Your Tools

A **map** is a picture that shows the location of things and places.

Looking at your map locate the following places:

1) Friendly Town businesses
2) Places to play
3) People's houses
4) Names of streets

b. Use colored pencils to color each of the locations with the following colors:

1) Friendly Town businesses – red
2) Places to play – green
3) People's houses – blue
4) Names of the streets – gray

c. Using your map make a list of at least two places for each category.

1) Friendly Town businesses ______________________

____

2) Places to play ______________________

____

3) People's houses ______________________

____

4) Names of streets ______________________

____

Day 2 a. On the map there are some crossed lines with some capital letters. This is called a compass. What do you think the four letters stand for?

____

____

b. Tell your teacher the directions for these trips:
1) Friendly Town Church to Mary's house
2) Bill's house to Happy Park
3) Lovely Lake to Sue's house
4) Piggy Bank to Town Post Office

c. Determine the direction (north, south, east, or west) of two or three places from your house.

____

____

____

____

____

____

d. Enrichment

Sometimes pairs of words are related to each other in the same way. These are called analogies.

Ex: mother : woman :: father : man

Mother is to *woman* as *father* is to what?

Write the answers to the following analogies.

Word Box		
neck	bird	hands
dog	hear	hand

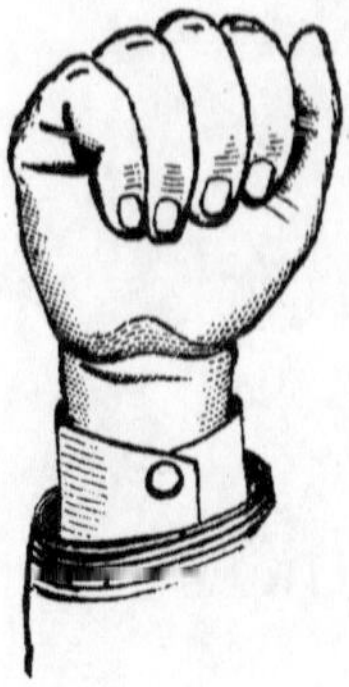

1) eyes : see :: ears : ________

2) socks : feet :: gloves : ________

3) sleeve : arm :: collar : ________

4) claw : bird :: paw : ________

5) nose : face :: finger : ________

6) water : fish :: air : ________

Day 3 a. Discussion with teacher.

b. Find at least one example for each of the following features on your state or town map.

1) river ________

2) park ________

3) mountain (or other landform) ________

4) airport ________

5) road ________

c. Discussion with teacher.

d. Enrichment

Sometimes pairs of words are related to each other in the same way. These are called analogies. Fill in the blank to make the analogy correct.

1) kitten : cat :: puppy : __________

2) bear : cub :: sheep : __________

3) calf : cow :: foal : __________

4) laugh : happy :: cry : __________

5) right : left :: east : __________

6) up : down :: north : __________

Word Box	
horse	lamb
south	sad
dog	west

Day 4 a. Proper nouns are specific people, places, or things. Proper nouns begin with a capital letter. Here are some examples: New York, Mrs. Jones, Friday. Show your teacher examples of specific places on your map.

How do the names of these places start?__________

Grammar Guide

A **proper noun** names a particular person, place, or thing. Begin a proper noun with a **capital letter**.

b. There are names of three specific people on the map of Friendly Town. Find their names on your map and underline them.

c. Write your entire name. __________

What kind of letter does your name start with? __________

What about your middle name? __________

d. Write two names for each category. Make sure they start with capital letters.

1) Days of the week __________ __________

2) Months __________ __________

3) Holidays __________ __________

4) Specific products you can buy __________

____

e. Enrichment

Sometimes pairs of words are related to each other in the same way. These are called analogies. Fill in the blank to make the analogy correct.

Word Box	
cold	hear
pear	furniture
chair	vegetable

1) grapes : fruit :: squash : __________

2) red : apple :: green : __________

3) stove : hot :: refrigerator : __________

4) sleep : bed :: sit : __________

5) pictures : see :: music : __________

6) dog : animal :: table : __________

Day 5 a. Choose a location on our Friendly Town map and draw your house.
Try to make your house about the same size as the other houses.
Think about where you would like to live before you choose your location.
Write your name, apostrophe and **s ('s)**, and the word *house* on the house.
Ex: Ron's house

b. Anyone can draw a map. With your teacher's help draw a map of your room or house in the space provided below. Decide the shape of the room or house and then draw in things like doors and windows. You may also add things like furniture, rugs, and lamps. It can be as simple or as detailed as you want it to be. It may also take several tries to make it look like you want it to, so don't get discouraged.

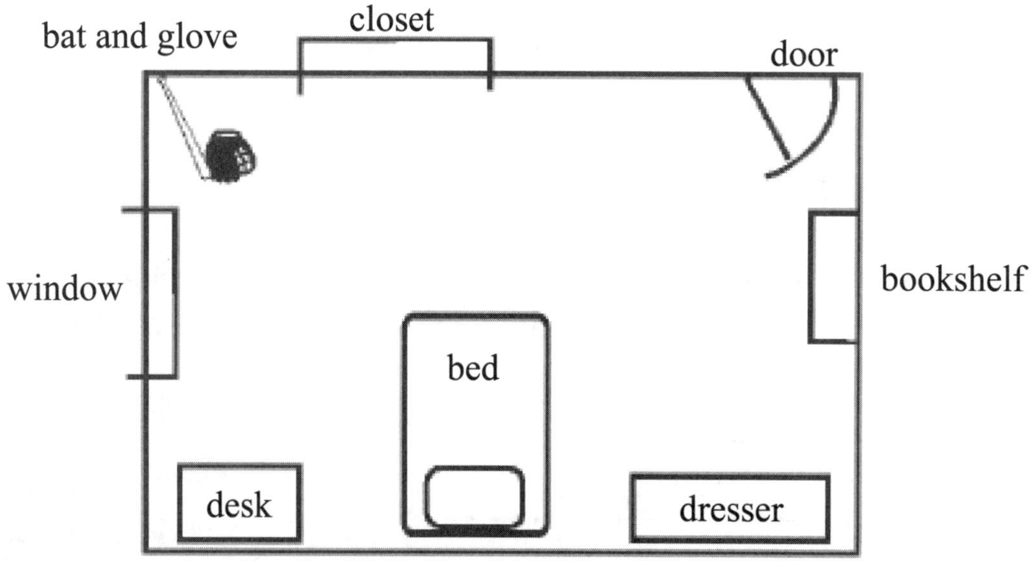

c. Journal Entry: Pretend you are taking someone on a tour of your room. Write what you would say on this tour.

Review Activities

1. Use the map from Lesson 14 to answer these questions.

   a. What is east of the Eiffel Tower? ____________________

   b. What is north of the Eiffel Tower? ____________________

2. Fill in the compass with north, south, east, and west.

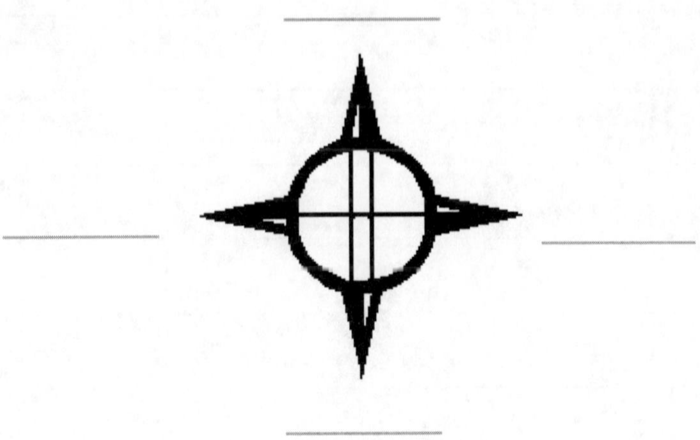

3. Write two proper nouns for each word.

   a. months ______________ ______________

   b. boy's names ______________ ______________

   c. cities ______________ ______________

4. Divide these words into syllables.

   a. slipper ________ b. people ________ c. circle ________ d. letter ________

Mowgli grew stronger as a boy must grow who lives in the jungle. Each day he learned many lessons and had nothing in the world to think of except things to eat.

The Jungle Book by Rudyard Kipling, 1894.

Day 1 a. Write the passage from dictation, or copy it. Compare your copy to the literature passage and make corrections.

b.

Focus on Spelling

please pleased pleasing grow growing

Bonus Word: jungle

Copy these spelling words. Say the words aloud as you write them.

c. Enrichment

Unscramble these letters to make your spelling words.

1) eealpds ________
2) orwg ________
3) gesilpan ________
4) goingwr ________
5) eelpsa ________

Day 2 a. Underline the word in your literature passage that ends with the suffix **-er**.

b. Look at the **-er** word from our literature passage.

Tell your teacher a rule for adding **-er** to a word ending in silent **e**.

Grammar Guide
To add **-er** to most words, just add **-er**. To add **-er** to a word ending with a silent **e**, drop the **e** and add **-er**.

c. Rewrite these words, adding the suffix **-er** to each word:

1) slow ________ 3) fast ________ 5) dark ________
2) ripe ________ 4) nice ________ 6) white ________

d. Fill in these sentences with the words you made in **2c**.

1) The tortoise is ________ than the hare, but he won the race.
2) The dark clouds became ________ as the storm approached.
3) Mary's banana is ________ than mine.
4) The weather is ________ today than yesterday.
5) The clean sheets look ________ than snow.
6) I can run ________ than Mom.

e. **SEE-SPELL-SAY:** Look and **see** each word on the spelling list. **Spell** each word aloud. **Say** the word.

Day 3 a. Discussion with teacher.

Grammar Guide
Pronoun - a word which takes the place of a noun

b. Pronouns are used in place of nouns. Find the pronoun in each sentence and underline it.

1) We will go to the park.
2) Are you and Mother going to the store?
3) She is wearing a blue dress.
4) Bring it into the house.
5) They are waiting for the next bus.
6) Please give the book to me.

c. Spelling Bee

d. Enrichment

Sometimes pairs of words are related to each other in the same way. These are called analogies. Fill in the blank to make the analogy correct.

Word Box	
winter	feet
cow	evening
cat	she

1) bark : dog :: purr : ____________

2) sunrise : sunset :: morning : ____________

3) eggs : hen :: milk : ____________

4) his : her :: he : ____________

5) hat : head :: shoes : ____________

6) swim : summer :: ski : ____________

Day 4 a. Discussion with teacher.

b – c. Discussion with teacher.

d. Spelling Pretest

e. Enrichment

Sometimes pairs of words are related to each other in the same way. These are called analogies. Fill in the blank to make the analogy correct.

Word Box			
should not		he will	I have
m	u	B	H

1) J : j :: M : __________

2) R : s :: T : __________

3) w : W :: b : __________

4) e : F :: g : __________

5) couldn't : could not :: shouldn't : __________

6) she'll : she will :: he'll : __________

7) they've : they have :: I've : __________

Day 5 a. Being able to read different kinds of charts and graphs is important. Here are three different kinds of charts and graphs with questions following each one.

First is a bar graph. It shows the number of oranges picked from the Smith family orange trees each year for four years. The height of each bar tells how many oranges were picked each year.

Oranges Picked from the Smiths' Trees

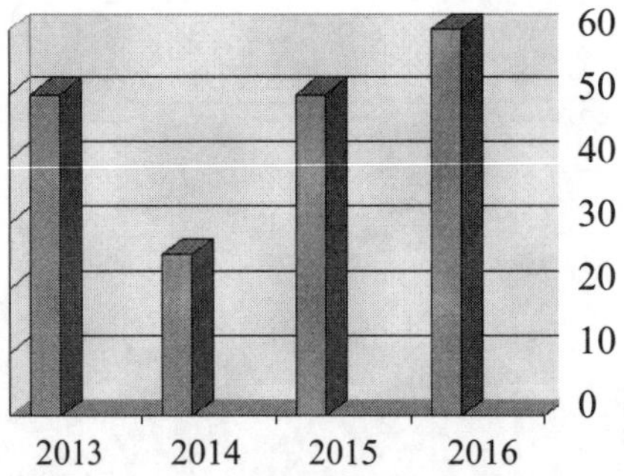

1) In what year were the most oranges picked? ______________

   How many oranges were picked that year? ______________

2) In what year were the lowest number of oranges picked? ______________

   How many oranges were picked? ______________

3) During two years the same number of oranges were picked.

   What years were they? ______________

   How many oranges were picked during those years?

   ____

4) Sometimes numbers don't tell the whole story. Can you think of reasons why the Smith family only picked 25 oranges in 2014? Come up with at least three possible answers.

____

____

____

____

____

____

____

b. Here is another kind of chart. It shows us how many times each member of the Smith family swam during their vacation. This chart uses tally marks. Tally marks are made in groups of five.

Here are four tally marks: ||||
Here are five tally marks: ~~||||~~

The fifth tally mark is made across the first four. That way when you count the marks you can count by groups of five.

Swimming Trips on the Smith's Vacation	
Dad	𝍸 𝍷𝍷𝍷𝍷
Mom	𝍸 𝍷𝍷𝍷
Sam	𝍸 𝍸 𝍸
Jill	𝍸 𝍸 𝍷𝍷𝍷𝍷
Mike	𝍸 𝍸 𝍷𝍷𝍷

1) Who went swimming the most times during the Smith family vacation? ______

   How many times did this person swim? ______

2) Who went swimming the least number of times during the Smith family vacation? ______

   How many times did this person swim? ______

3) How many times did the boys (Dad included) swim? ______

   How many times did Jill and Mom swim altogether? ______

4) Think about fun things you can do at a lake or the ocean. List at least three activities the Smith family may have done on their vacation by the water. Tell why you think Sam Smith went swimming so many times.

______

______

______

______

______

______

______

c. This type of graph uses pictures to show the numbers it is reporting. The Smith children have a little business. They make and sell yo-yos. This graph shows the design or color and number of yo-yos they made.

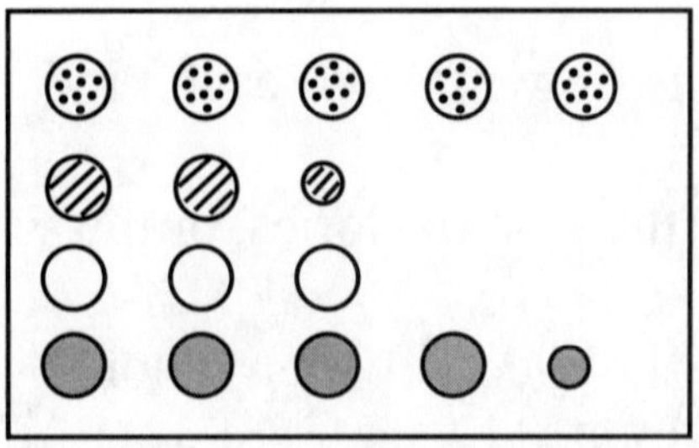

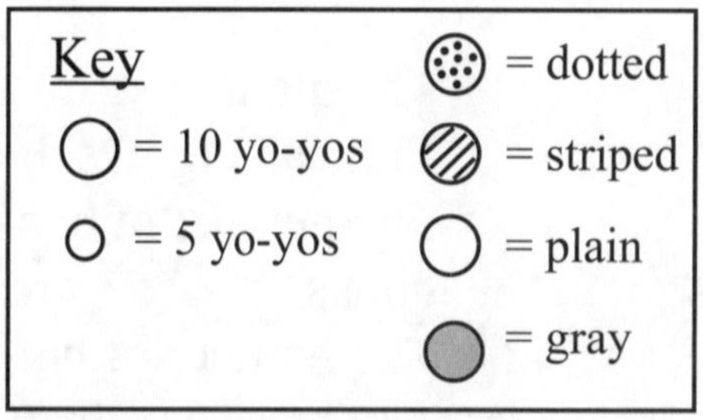

1) What kind of yo-yo did the Smiths make the most? ____________

How many of this type did they make? ____________

2) What kind of yo-yo did the Smiths make the least? ____________

How many of this type yo-yo did they make? ____________

3) How many striped and plain yo-yos did they make altogether?

____

How many yo-yos did they make altogether? ____________

4) Why do you think the dotted yo-yo sold best? ____________

____

Do you think this would be a fun business for three children to have? ____________________________

Tell your teacher what kind of business you might like to have.

____

d. Using the space provided make your own graph or chart. There are many things you can tell about with a chart or graph. With your teacher's help choose something you can tell about using this method. Here are some suggestions:

1) The main kinds of toys you have and how many of each kind. Ex: cars, trucks, boats, etc.
2) The number of books you have and the type of stories, or the size of the books
3) The number of houses on your street divided by their colors
4) The number of cars on your street divided by their colors

e. Spelling Test

______________________	______________________
______________________	______________________
______________________	______________________

f. Journal Entry: Complete this thought: Last year I could not

______________________, but now I can.

g. Handwriting: Connecting Letters
Some letters connect together very easily. If a letter has a tail that swoops up from the bottom line, then it is easy to connect it to some letters. Practice these connections.

am

at

an

as

al

em

et

en

es

el

im

it

in

is

il

Review Activities

1. Add the suffix **-er**.

a. nice ____________ c. ripe ____________

b. tall ____________ d. wise ____________

2. Circle the pronouns.

a. He is early for dinner.

b. Mom and I cooked chicken.

c. They will bring rolls.

3. Read the graph and answer the questions.

Cupcakes Decorated	
Anne	𝍸 𝍸 /
Emily	𝍸 𝍸 𝍸 /
Michael	𝍸 //
Quen	𝍸 ///

a. Who decorated the most cupcakes? ____________

b. How many did he or she decorate? ____________

c. Who decorated the least cupcakes? ____________

d. How many did he or she decorate? ____________

e. How many cupcakes did Anne and Emily decorate altogether?

____

f. How many cupcakes did Quen and Michael decorate altogether?

____

Assessment 4

(Lessons 15 – 17)

1. Read these sentences and decide which sentence needs an apostrophe. Write the apostrophe.

   a. The *dogs* like the food.

   b. Bring in the *dogs* food.

   c. The hats are for the *boys*.

   d. These are the *boys* hats.

2. List two facts about yourself.

   ____

   ____

3. Write two proper nouns for each word.

   a. holidays ______________________

   b. days of the week ______________________

   c. states ______________________

4. Add the suffix **-er** to these words.

   a. hard ____________ c. nice ____________

   b. white ____________ d. soft ____________

5. Circle the pronouns.

    a. They are happy.
    b. We like cake.
    c. She is nice.
    d. I am in a hurry.

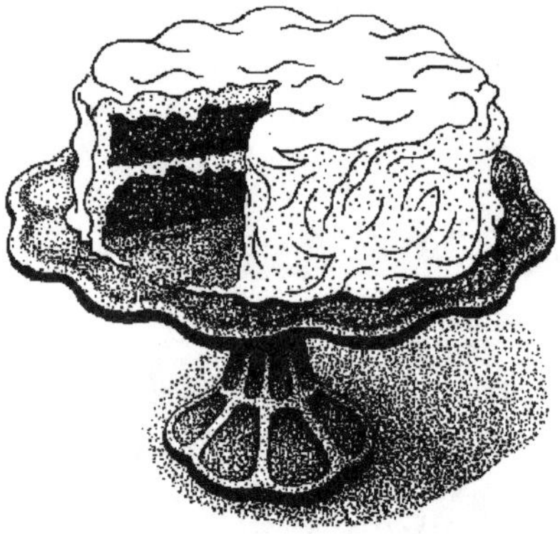

6. Divide these words into syllables.

a. option ____________	c. illusion ____________
b. reluctant ____________	d. adventure ____________

LITERATURE LINK

Day 1 Listen to your teacher read the vocabulary words.

Vocabulary

soldier	important	special	president
Continental	American	honest	plantation
surveyor	Revolution	government	wealthy

Discussion with teacher.

Begin reading the story "George Washington's Journey." You will have time tomorrow to finish the story.

George Washington's Journey

George Washington was a man who was very important to America. He was special for many reasons. He was the first president of our country. He led our army during the American Revolution. We think of him as the "Father of Our Country." Why was George Washington so special? It was the way he did great things. He was very brave and honest. He made other people feel important, too.

George was born on February 22, 1732 in Virginia. His father was a wealthy owner of a big plantation. George loved to play outside as a boy, and he liked to play sports. His favorite thing to do was to ride horses. He became a very good rider. Life was good for George until his father died when he was eleven.

George moved to a place called Mount Vernon to live with his older brother Lawrence. As he grew he learned to do many things. When he was fourteen he learned how to be a surveyor and went to the unsettled parts of our country. He saw Indians and lots of new things.

He was happy again until his brother Lawrence died when George was twenty. At this time George joined the army. He became a very good soldier. He was helpful to his army. He fought with the English Army in the French and Indian War. In 1759 George married Martha Custis. She was a young widow with two children. George and Martha lived at Mount Vernon. George was happy taking care of his family and home.

In 1775 George again became a soldier. He was asked to be the leader of the Continental Army. This was the army of the thirteen colonies. This army had to fight the strong English Army. They were mostly just farmers and men from the woods. The people wanted to be free from the English king. The army led by General Washington had many hard times. They didn't have enough food or warm clothes, but George kept them together. After six years of fighting, the Continental Army won. In 1781 the war was over and the colonies were free.

George thought his work was over, so he went home to Mount Vernon. The young government of America was having trouble, so George went to Philadelphia to help. He helped write the Constitution. In 1789 he was elected the first president. He was president for eight years. He helped people learn how to work together and helped the government get started. George Washington was a good president.

In 1797 George went back home to Mount Vernon. He had served his country well. He had been a good soldier and leader. George Washington died December 14, 1799. Many people loved and honored him. They thought he was a brave and honest leader. The people wanted to honor all that he did for America. They named the capital city after him, Washington, D.C.

Day 2 a. Finish reading the book or story from yesterday.

b. **Discussion Questions for "George Washington's Journey" or *Meet George Washington*:**

1) When and where was George Washington born?
2) What was life like while George Washington's father was alive? What were George's favorite things to do as a boy?
3) When George was only fourteen he began to work. What job did he do? How did life change again for George when he was twenty?
4) When George became a soldier what army did he fight with? What was the first war he fought in?
5) What was George Washington's wife's name? Where did he and his family go to live?
6) In 1775 Washington became the head of a new army. What country did he fight for then? What kind of army did General Washington have to fight with?
7) General Washington showed his bravery and leadership many times. Finally, the American Revolution ended. What year did it end?
8) What was his last and very important job for his country? When did George Washington become our first president? How long did he remain president? What is the special name given to George Washington?

c. Match the events with the dates. Look back in your story if you need help doing this activity.

Event	***Date***
1) George Washington is born.	1743
2) George's father dies.	1752
3) George takes command of the Continental Army.	1775
4) George Washington dies.	1799
5) George's brother, Lawrence, dies.	1789
6) George is elected president.	1732
7) George marries Martha Custis.	1759

d. Answer the following questions about George's life:

1) How old was George Washington when he died? ____________

2) How old was he when he was married? ____________

3) How old was he when he became the leader of the Continental Army? ____________

4) How old was George Washington when he became the first president? ____________

Day 3 a. Below is a list of activities done by George Washington. Use the letters below to indicate when in his life these activities may have been done.

B – Boyhood Years (0 – 12 years old)
Y – Young Man (13 – 21 years old)
M – Mature (Grown-Up) Man (22 – 50 years old)
O – Older Years (over 50 years old)

1) George became a surveyor. ____________

2) George liked to play outside and ride horses. ____________

3) George married Martha Custis. ____________

4) George became our first president. ____________

5) George's father died. ____________

6) George became a soldier in the English Army. ____________

7) George was made leader of the Continental Army. ____________

8) George's army defeated the English to end the American Revolution. ____________

9) George returned to Mount Vernon after being president.

____

10) George's brother, Lawrence, died. ____________

b. Look up these words in the dictionary or online. Discuss the meanings with your teacher and write a brief definition for each of them:

1) hero ______________________________

2) leader ______________________________

3) brave ______________________________

4) honest ______________________________

5) discipline ______________________________

6) dignity ______________________________

c. Tell how you think each of these words could apply to George Washington. Do you think these are good words to describe him?

____

d. Fill in the blanks with one of these words

hero leader brave honest discipline dignity

1) When George Washington would not tell a lie, he showed that he was ______________________.

2) When a soldier goes into battle, even if he is afraid, he must be ______________________.

3) When they needed a general for the army they knew George would be a good ______________________.

4) George's ______________________ showed when he worked hard, did not use bad language, and told the truth.

5) After the Revolutionary War was over everyone thought George was a ______________________.

6) The way George was fair and quietly led people by his actions showed great ______________.

Day 4. a. A story was written about George Washington after his death. It told about an experience George may have had as a boy. As the story goes, George cut down his father's cherry tree with his hatchet. When his father asked him about it George said, "I can not tell a lie. I chopped down the cherry tree." The story then tells that George's father hugged him. Since we don't know whether or not it is true, we can call it a legend about George Washington.

Answer these questions about this story:

1) Have you ever heard this story about George Washington?

____

2) What do you think is important about what George did in this story? _______________

3) Why do you think his father hugged him? _______________

____

4) Do you think George did the right thing? What would you have done? _______________

____

5) This story points out a quality that George Washington had that made him a very good leader. What was that quality?

____

b. On a separate piece of paper draw a picture or pictures to show what happened in this story about George as a young boy. Make sure to include his hatchet (a small ax) and the cherry tree. These two things are symbols of this story.

c. Copy this Scripture on the back of your picture. Read it to your teacher, and discuss its meaning:

Do not let kindness and truth leave you;
Bind them around your neck,
Write them on the tablet of your heart.
So you will find favor and good repute
In the sight of God and man.

Proverbs 3:3 – 4 (NASB)

Day 5. a. You are going to give a presentation on George Washington. Use your activities and any pictures you drew or found to help you tell the story of his life. To prepare for your presentation you may answer the following questions.

1) Who was George Washington?
2) What important things happened in his life?
3) Why is it important to know about George Washington?
4) What is your favorite part of George Washington's life?
5) What did you learn from George Washington?

b. Handwriting
Here are some more letters which connect together easily. The letters do not change. That is why they are easy to connect. Practice these connections:

uh

up

uk

uf

uj

ah

ap

ak

af

aj

ha

pa

ka

fa

ja

I **C.A.N.** Assessment
Literature Link on *George Washington*

After the Literature Link on *George Washington* is completed check off each I **C.A.N.** objective with your teacher.

______	**C**	I can **complete** my work.
______		I can be **creative**.
______	**A**	I can be **accurate**.
______		I can do my work with a good **attitude**.
______	**N**	I can do my work **neatly**.

Notes

EVERYDAY WORDS

Alice: *Would you tell me, please, which way I ought to go from here?*

Cheshire Cat: (smiling) *That depends a good deal on where you want to get to.*

Alice: *I don't much care where -*

Cheshire Cat: (interrupting) *Then it doesn't matter which way you go!*

This playlet is taken from *Alice's Adventures in Wonderland* by Lewis Carroll, 1904

Day 1 a. Listen as your teacher reads the sentences, called lines.
Read the lines with her as she reads them a second time.
Copy these lines from the model.

b.

Focus on Spelling

thought bought brought fought ought

Bonus Word: would

Copy these spelling words. Say the words aloud as you write them.

c. Enrichment

Fill in the blanks to make your spelling words.

1) 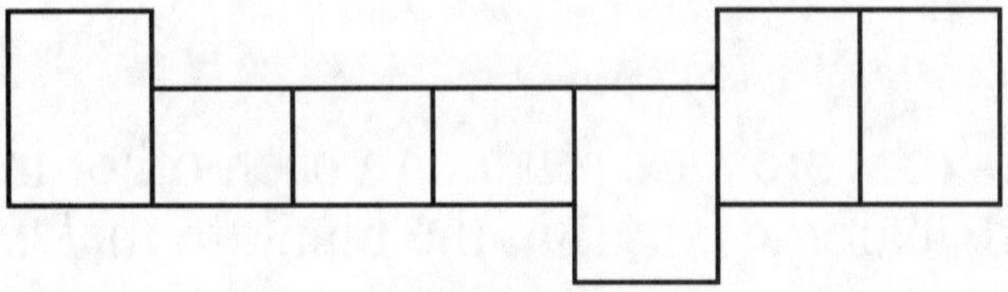

2) 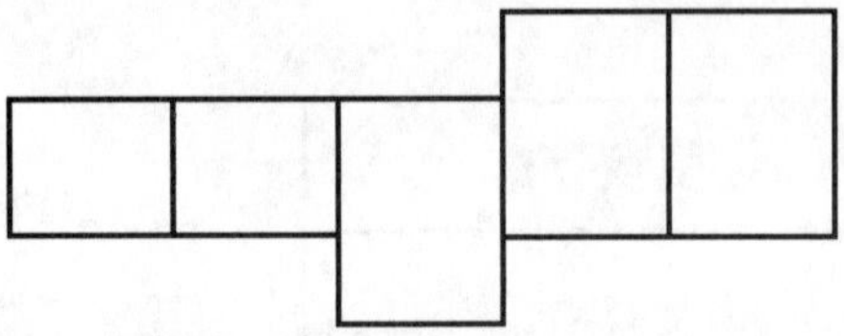

3) 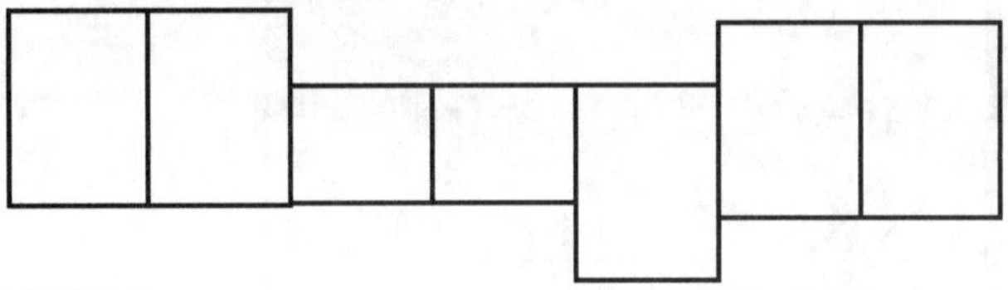

4) 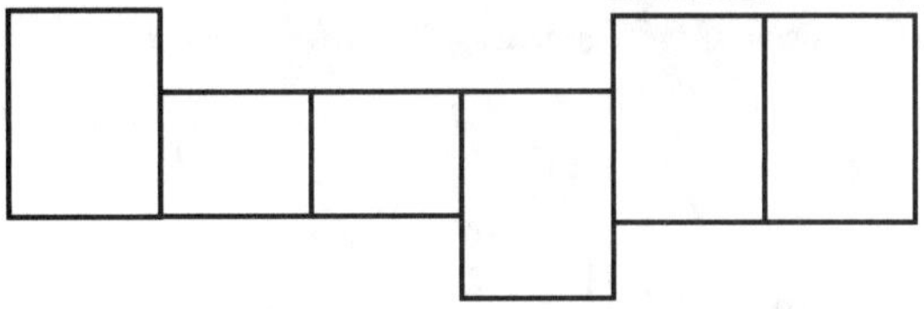

5) 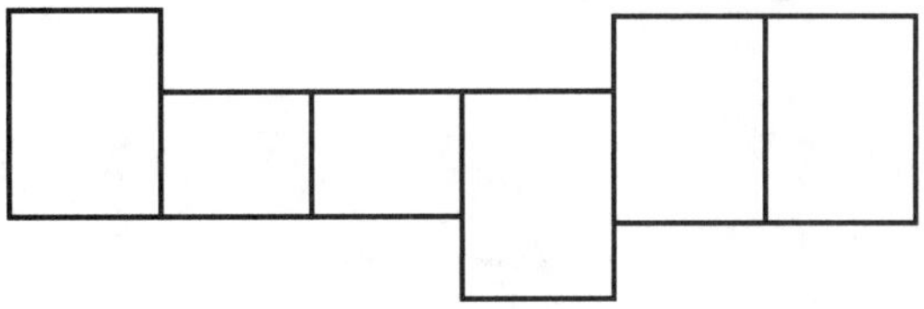

Day 2 a. Underline in red the names of the people in the play.

Who are the characters in this play?

Punctuation Pointer
Colon - a colon (**:**) is used in a play after a character's name and before his lines.

b. Find the stage directions and underline them in blue.

c. Using two different colors (yellow and green), underline the words spoken by the characters. Underline in yellow the words spoken by Alice and the words spoken by the Cheshire Cat in green.

d. Discussion with teacher.

e. **SEE-SPELL-SAY:** Look and **see** each word on the spelling list. **Spell** each word aloud. **Say** the word.

f. Enrichment

Sometimes pairs of words are related to each other in the same way. These are called analogies. Fill in the blank to make the analogy correct.

Word Box	
they'll	no one
aren't	measure
mouse	didn't

1) must not : mustn't :: did not : ____________________

2) we will : we'll :: they will : ____________________

3) is not : isn't :: are not : ____________________

4) pounds : weigh :: inch : ____________________

5) children : child :: mice : ____________________

6) everything : nothing :: everyone : ____________________

Day 3 a. What punctuation ends each sentence in the play?

____________ ____________ ____________

b. Write a sentence ending in an question mark **(?)**.

____

c. Write a sentence ending in a period **(.)**.

____

____

d. Discussion with teacher.

e. Write a sentence ending in an exclamation point **(!)**.

____

f. Write a sentence that gives a command.

____

g. Add the correct punctuation to the following sentences:

1. The Rabbit noticed Alice
2. Why, Mary, Ann, what are you doing here
3. Run home this moment and fetch me a pair of gloves
4. Alice was so frightened that she ran off at once

h. Enrichment

Sometimes pairs of words are related to each other in the same way. These are called analogies. Fill in the blank to make the analogy correct.

Word Box	
date	stopping
read	tennis
swim	noun

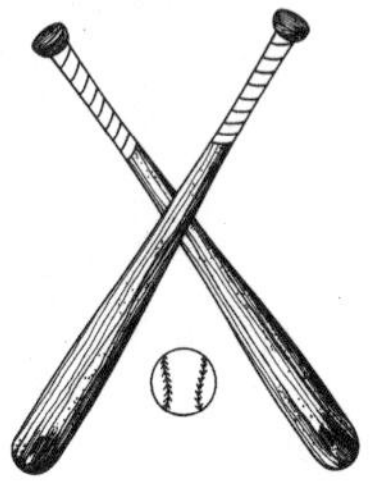

1) run : verb :: boy : ____________

2) sit : sitting :: stop : ____________

3) clock : time :: calendar : ____________

4) snow : ski :: water : ____________

5) bat : baseball :: racquet : ____________

6) pen : write :: book : ____________

Day 4 a. Read the following short play.

Optional Props: chair, jacket, bag, blanket, jar, container

Visit to the Pond

Mother: (sitting in a chair) Well, it's almost time for spring.

Ann: (sitting by her mother) Yes, it's a wonderful, sunny day.

David: (jumps up and down in an excited way) Oh, Mother, let's walk down to the pond!

Mother: (stands up and looks out the window) Yes, children, you are right. It is a good day to be outside. We will go down to the pond.

Ann: Yay! (claps her hands and puts on her jacket)

David: I will bring bread to feed to the ducks and fish. (holds up bag)

Ann: I will bring a jar to catch minnows. (holds up container)

Mother: I will bring a blanket to sit on. Come on, let's go! (They walk out together.)

b. There are three characters in this play. Underline the name of each character with these colors:

Mother	–	yellow
Ann	–	green
David	–	blue

Underline the stage directions for each character in red.

c. Now go back and underline the words spoken by each character in their own color. (You may want to use highlighter markers instead of crayons or colored pencils.)

d. Choose parts and read the play.

e. Spelling Pretest

f. Enrichment
Sometimes pairs of words are related to each other in the same way. These are called analogies. Fill in the blank to make the analogy correct.

Word Box	
grandfather	stop
unhappy	hungry
throw	finish

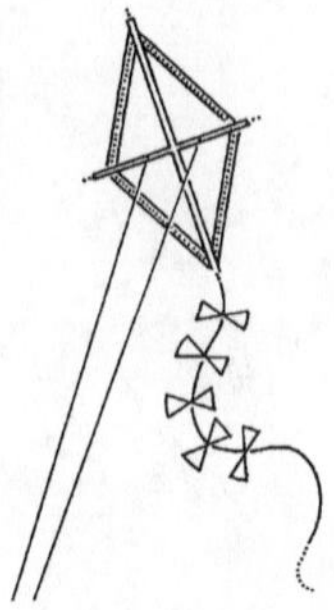

1) kite : fly :: ball : ____________

2) drink : thirsty :: eat : ____________

3) bride : groom :: grandmother : ____________

4) green : go :: red : ____________

5) happy : glad :: sad : ____________

6) begin : start :: end : ____________

Day 5 a. – d. Discussion with teacher.

e. Spelling Test

f. Journal Entry: Think of a conversation you had with someone recently. Write it in play form.

g. Handwriting

pup

sun

fun

ten

men

tip

sit

rip

nut

hut

let

hem

set

him

fin

Review Activities

1. Read this section of a play and answer the following questions.

Ryan: (wiping his eyes) I can't find my puppy.
Jason: (putting his arm around Ryan) Let's go look for him together.
Ryan: I've already looked for him. (sobbing)
Jason: We will keep trying until we find him.

a. Who are the characters in the play?

____

b. Circle the colon that follows each character's lines.

c. Underline the stage directions.

2. Circle the pronouns.

a. She is going to the movie.

b. I am going with her.

c. They will be late.

3. Add the suffix **–er** to each word.

a. small ____________________

b. large ____________________

c. ripe ____________________

d. tall ____________________

4. Look at the play in question number 1. Underline the contractions in red.

"When I used to read fairy tales, I thought that kind of thing never happened and here I am in the middle of one!" Alice said, "There ought to be a book written about me. When I grow up, I will write one."

Alice's Adventures in Wonderland by
Lewis Carroll, 1865

Day 1 a. Write the last sentence from dictation, or copy it. Compare your copy to the literature passage and make corrections.

b.

Focus on Spelling

write wrap wreck wrote wrong

Bonus Word: happened

Copy these spelling words. Say the words aloud as you write them.

c. Enrichment

Find your spelling words in this puzzle: wrong wrap write wrote wreck

w	r	o	n	g	m	b
r	w	b	o	v	e	a
a	r	q	g	w	t	l
p	o	w	r	i	t	e
b	t	h	i	n	d	n
y	e	w	r	e	c	k

Day 2 a. Read the literature passage and underline in blue the words spoken by Alice.

b. With a blue pencil circle the quotation marks in the literature passage.

Punctuation Pointer
Quotation marks are placed around the actual spoken words.

c. Look at the last sentence of the literature passage. A comma (,) comes before the opening quotation mark. With a green pencil circle this comma. What punctuation comes before the closing quotation mark?

____

d. Place quotation marks around the actual words spoken.

1) John said, Come play basketball with me.

2) Mary asked, What time is Abbey getting home?

3) Mother replied, She will be home pretty soon.

e. Remember that the first word of a quotation begins with a capital letter.

Correct the following sentences by adding capitalization.

1) Eric asked, “why is tennis such a noisy sport?”

2) The boys replied, “we don’t know.”

3) Eric laughed, “because everyone raises a racket!”

Grammar Guide

Begin the first word of a quotation with a **capital letter**.

f. Complete the following quotation.

Mother asked, "What would you like for dessert?"

________________ said, "______________________________."
(*Your name*)

g. Try writing your own quotation.

____

____

h. **SEE-SPELL-SAY:** Look and **see** each word on the spelling list. **Spell** each word aloud. **Say** the word.

Day 3 a. Look at the last sentence in our literature passage. Who is the sentence about? In red underline the word that tells whom the sentence is about. This word tells us the subject of the sentence.

Grammar Guide

Complete sentence - expresses a complete thought

Grammar Guide

Subject – tells who or what the sentence is about
Predicate – tells something about the subject

b. In blue underline the words that tell us what Alice wants to do when she grows up. This part of the sentence is called the predicate.

c. Look at the sentence below. Underline in red the words that name what the sentence is about. Underline in blue the words that tell something about what was named.

The cat is black and white.

d. Read each sentence. Underline the subject of the sentence in red. Underline the predicate, or part that tells about the subject, in blue.

1) My dog is jumping and barking.

2) Mother went to the store.

3) I like to eat ice cream.

4) The boat is floating in the water.

5) Bill can play with the toys.

6) Dad likes to go camping.

e. Spelling Bee

f. Enrichment

Sometimes pairs of words are related to each other in the same way. These are called analogies. Fill in the blank to make the analogy correct.

Word Box	
apple	forest
cold	horn
sew	vegetable

1) wood : build :: cloth : ____________________

2) strum : guitar :: blow : ____________________

3) coffee : hot :: juice : ____________________

4) pie : dessert :: broccoli : ____________________

5) yellow : lemon :: red : ____________________

6) cow : farm :: raccoon : ____________________

Day 4 a. Find the word in your literature passage that ends with **-ed**.

b. Find the words in your literature passage that can complete these sentences.

1) Today, I think. Yesterday, I ____________.

2) Today, I ____________. Yesterday, I wrote.

c. Match each word with the correct word that shows it has already happened:

Today, I...	**Yesterday, I...**
talk	made
run	baked
bake	talked
make	jumped
jump	ran
smile	thought
think	smiled

d. Fill in the following blanks using the words in the box.

made	baked	talked	jumped
ran	thought	smiled	

1) We were hungry, so we ____________ cookies.

2) The frog ____________ out of the bucket.

3) The boy with the ball ____________ for a touchdown.

4) I ____________ at my new baby sister.

5) We came home because we ____________ it was time for dinner.

6) When Grandma called on the phone I ____________ to her.

7) After I got up I ____________ my bed.

e.. Spelling Pretest

______________________ ______________________

______________________ ______________________

______________________ ______________________

Day 5 a. Replace the italicized word(s) with the correct pronoun in the box.

They He She We It

1) *Bill* went to the store. ______________ went to the store.

2) *Mother* washed the dishes. ______________ washed the dishes.

3) *Bill and Bob* played ball. ______________ played ball.

4) *Sally and I* rode our bikes. ______________ rode our bikes.

5) *The car* is in the road. ______________ is in the road.

b. Write three sentences about yourself and begin each with the word *I*.

____

____

____

____

____

____

c. Underline the pronouns used in each sentence:

1) They brought a cake for the party.

2) We are going to visit Grandma.

3) Please put it back.

4) She likes to grow flowers in the garden.

5) I helped build the birdhouse.

6) The game will start when he comes.

d. Rewrite the following paragraph using pronouns for the italicized words. Remember to indent the first sentence.

Mom and I are very happy. *Mom and I* are going on a trip to the lake. We will go boating on *the lake*. Dad is coming, too. *Dad* likes to camp. Mom and Dad are happy to go on this trip. *Mom and Dad* are ready for a fun time. Mom is calling. *Mom* says it's time to go. Goodbye!

e. Spelling Test

f. Enrichment

Sometimes pairs of words are related to each other in the same way. These are called analogies. Fill in the blank to make the analogy correct.

Word Box		
3	catch	double
4	uncle	twice

1) first : 1 :: fourth : ____________
2) twins : 2 :: triplets : ____________
3) 1 : once :: 2 : ____________
4) niece : nephew :: aunt : ____________
5) pitcher : pitch :: catcher : ____________
6) 1 : single :: 2 : ____________

g. Journal Entry: Make a list of relatives you know well. Choose one to describe.

h. Handwriting

rut

fur

hurt

surf

twin

tent

rest

sell

nets

pens

hill

sits

lift

ring

tiny

Review Activities

1. Place quotation marks around the actual words spoken.

   a. Steve yelled, Look outside!

   b. Casey exclaimed, It's snowing!

   c. Mom asked, What's going on?

2. Rewrite these sentences, adding capitalization.

   a. James asked, "may I have another cookie?"

   ____

   b. Mother replied, "you may have one more cookie."

   ____

3. Circle the subject and underline the predicate.

   a. The boy chased the dog.

   b. The big dog ran under the fence.

   c. The cat climbed a tall tree.

   d. The kitten hid in the bushes.

4. Match the verb on the left to the verb on the right that shows it has already happened.

a. talk	made
b. think	ran
c. make	smiled
d. smile	talked
e. run	thought

5. Rewrite the sentences replacing the nouns with the correct pronoun.

a. *Sandy and Eric* came to my house.

____

b. *Sara, Eric, and I* played bingo.

____

c. *Sara* won the game.

____

d. *The game* was fun.

____

Notes

Alice was getting very tired of sitting and having nothing to do. She wanted to make a daisy chain but was not sure it was worth the trouble of getting up and picking the daisies. Suddenly she watched a Rabbit with pink eyes run close by her.

Alice's Alice in Wonderland by Lewis Carroll, 1965

Day 1 a. Copy the passage. Compare your copy to the literature passage and make corrections.

b. Discussion with teacher.

Day 2 a. Review the spelling lists in Lessons 15, 17, 19, and 20.

b. Enrichment

Fill in the blanks using a word that begins with **sw**.

1) The candy tastes ____________.

2) I will learn to ____________ in the pool.

3) There are ducks and ____________ on the lake.

Fill in the blanks using a word that begins with **th**.

4) My pencil is long and ______________________.

5) I must use my brain to ______________________.

6) Twenty and ten equals ______________________.

c. Spelling

______________________ ______________________

______________________ ______________________

______________________ ______________________

______________________ ______________________

d. Writing from dictation

1) ____

____

2) ____

____

e. Discussion with teacher.

1) ____

____

2) ____

____

f. Enrichment

Write a noun in each sentence.

1) The ______________________ hits.

2) The ______________________ runs.

3) The ______________________ yells.

4) The ______________________________ swims.

5) The ______________________________ dives.

6) The ______________________________ splashes.

Day 3 a. There are three sounds that **-ed** can make at the end of a word:

1) /**ed**/ as in the word, *pointed*
2) /**t**/ as in the word, *boxed*
3) /**d**/ as in the word, *yelled.*

Phonics Fact

-ed at the end of a word can say /**ed**/ as in *pointed*, /**t**/ as in *boxed*, and /**d**/ as in *yelled.*

Read these words for your teacher and listen to the ending sound:

painted	waited	boxed
baked	yelled	dried

b. Circle the word in the literature passage where the **-ed** at the end says /**t**/ as in *baked.* Underline the word in your sentences where the **-ed** at the end says /**d**/ as in *yelled.* Draw a box around the word in your sentences where the **-ed** at the end says /**ed**/ as in *pointed.*

c. Read the following list of words to your teacher. Write /**t**/, /**d**/, or /**ed**/ beside each word, telling which sound the **-ed** at the end makes:

seated ________	mixed ________	waved ________
backed ________	followed ________	grounded ________
ended ________	benched ________	cleaned ________
stayed ________	graded ________	cracked ________
needed ________	passed ________	called ________

d. Choose one word from each column and make up a sentence using that word. You may do this orally or in writing.

Day 4 a. Discussion with teacher.

b. Write three or four sentences about your favorite part of Alice's adventures or write about an unusual adventure you would like to experience.

c. Enrichment

Think of verbs, or doing words, to complete these sentences.

1) A boy ________________________________.

2) A girl ________________________________.

3) A man ________________________________.

4) The lady ______________________________.

5) The dog ______________________________.

6) The baby _____________________________.

Day 5 a. Listen to your teacher read the vocabulary words for the story "Gone Fishing."

Vocabulary				
arrive	finally	excited	surround	
reflection	bass	bait	bream	wonder

b. Read the story to your teacher.

Gone Fishing

When I was a young boy my family lived with another family in a big house in the city. Our families had fun times together, and I had fun with a little girl in the other family named Michelle. Michelle and I were best friends.

One day my mother told me that Michelle and her family were moving away. They were moving to the country. My mother said that I wouldn't be able to see the family very much anymore. I was very sad, but Michelle told me that I would be able to come and visit her family in the summer.

That year it felt as if summer would never arrive. When it finally came I was so excited. I was going to spend a whole week in the country with my best friend. It was a long drive, but it was worth it to see Michelle and her new home. She lived on a lake surrounded by tall pine trees. Being from the city I had never seen such a pretty blue lake with tall grass growing around the banks. The water was so clear and blue, and the sun made a sparkling reflection dance across the water. As Michelle and I peered down into the water from her dock we could see large bass swimming slowly around the grass at the bottom of the lake.

Michelle's father had just bought her and her sisters fishing poles, so we decided to go fishing that afternoon. All we had for bait was pieces of bread, but we knew we would have fun even if we didn't catch anything. But as soon as we tossed in our hooks little bream (a small freshwater fish) began to attack our bait. We both sat with wide-eyed wonder at the dozens of little fish that seemed to have come from out of nowhere! Soon, as often happens on hot summer afternoons, it started to rain. It began to rain so hard we could hardly see. So we sat there, Michelle and I, laughing at the rain and smiling at the fish.

That day Michelle and I became even better friends. We were given a memory that kept our friendship together, even though we could not be together anymore. It's a fishing trip that has become stuck in my mind. I can still remember that clear blue lake, even though it has long since dried up, and I can still remember my smiling friend, even though she has moved away. Looking back I think perhaps it was our happiness that made that lake so blue and beautiful.

c. **Discussion Questions:**

1) Where did the two families live together?
2) What happened to Michelle and her family? How did this make the child feel?
3) What did Michelle tell her friend before she left?
4) Describe Michelle's new home.
5) What did Michelle and her friend do together?
6) What happened as they were fishing?
7) What does the author say about why the lake looked so blue?

d. Enrichment

Read the word on the left. By changing only the first letter of the word, fill in the blank of the sentence with the correct word.

1) brown Many jewels were on the king's ________________.
2) cook I will read my ________________.
3) matter Please mix the ________________.
4) found Mom bought a ________________ of butter.
5) dollar I put a tie on my ________________.
6) tough The carpenter sanded the ________________ wood.

e. Journal Entry: Describe a fun adventure you had with a friend or relative.

f. Handwriting

mo

so

ho

no

to

ma

pa

la

ha

ta

ac

ic

uc

ec

Review Activities

1. Add the suffix **-ed** to these words. Say the words aloud and decide if the word says **/t/**, **/d/**, or **/ed/**.

   a. lift ____________________ d. play ____________________

   b. yell ____________________ e. point ____________________

   c. jump ____________________ f. fix ____________________

2. Place quotation marks around the actual words spoken.

   a. Ryan yelled, Come with me!

   b. Mom said, Please come with me

   c. Grandma asked, Who has the paper?

3. Write the past tense verb for each one listed.
   Ex: talk – talked

   a. make ____________________ c. smile ____________________

   b. run ____________________ d. think ____________________

4. Replace the nouns with the correct pronoun. Write the pronoun in the blank.

   a. *Sarah and Eric* went to the park. ____________________

   b. *Sarah*, *Eric*, *and I* went to the movies. ____________________

   c. *Tina* called me yesterday. ____________________

"Oh, dear! I'm late!" yelled the Rabbit as he took a watch out of his waistcoat pocket and looked at it. Alice jumped to her feet, as she realized she had never seen a rabbit with either a waistcoat pocket or a watch to take out of it.

Alice's Adventures in Wonderland
by Lewis Carroll, 1865

Day 1 a. Write the first sentence of the literature passage from dictation. Compare your copy to the literature passage and make corrections.

b. Underline the words that were spoken by the Rabbit. How do you think he said them?

c. Draw a picture of the scene from the passage.

d. Enrichment

1) Mr. Dot wants to walk around this square. Using the words *up*, *down*, *right*, and *left*, give him directions to go around the square clockwise.

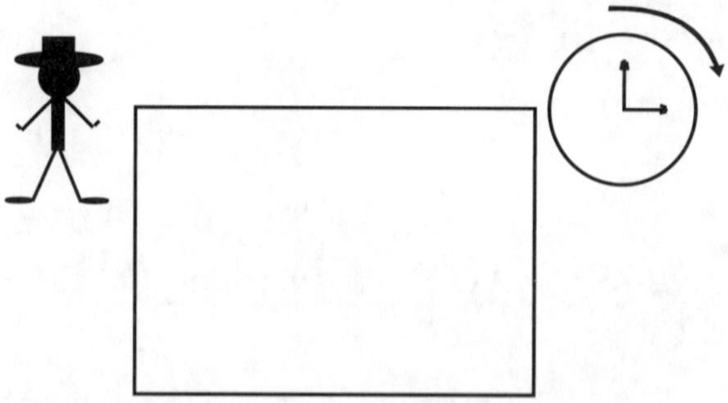

First, go ____________________.

Second, go ____________________.

Third, go ____________________.

Then go ____________________.

2) Now help Mr. Dot walk around the same square, counter-clockwise, using the words *up*, *down*, *right*, and *left*.

First, go ____________________.

Second, go ____________________.

Third, go ____________________.

Then go ____________________.

Day 2 a. Review the spelling lists in Lessons 1 – 20.

b. Spell the words for your teacher.

c. Writing from dictation

1) ______________________________

____

____

2) ______________________________

____

____

d. Discussion with teacher.

1) ______________________________

____

____

2) ______________________________

____

____

e. Enrichment

Read the list of words and write the word that comes next.

Ex: yesterday today <u>tomorrow</u>

1) breakfast lunch ______________

2) first second ______________

3) fall winter ______________

4) morning noon ______________

5) January February ______________

6) baby teenager ______________

Day 3 a. Find four words in your literature passage that end with the suffix **-ed**. Write each word. Tell your teacher what happened to the silent **e** when you added **-ed**.

____

____

b. Find the word in our literature passage that fills in the blank:

Today, I *take*. Yesterday, I ____________________.

c. Match these words with the words that show it has already happened:

Today, I...	**Yesterday, I...**
feel	told
pay	took
begin	ate
keep	felt
tell	found
take	began
find	paid
eat	kept

d. Fill in the following blanks using the words in the box:

told	took	ate	felt
began	paid	kept	found

1) The boys ____________________ an old baseball in the dirt.

2) We ____________________ school in the fall.

3) After I washed his car Mr. Smith ____________________ me.

4) When the cake was baked we ____________________ a big piece.

5) Dad ____________________ us not to play near the street.

6) My dad ______________________ his old baseball cards.

7) During the summer my family ______________________ a trip.

8) Mom ______________________ tired after a long day of work.

Day 4 a. Discussion with teacher.

b. Read the passage using a different voice spoken by Rabbit. What marks helped you know the words spoken? ____________________

c.

Punctuation Pointer Review
Quotation marks are placed around the actual spoken words.

Add quotation marks around the actual words spoken.

1) Jamie asked his friends, What has eight wheels and flies?

2) His friends replied, We don't know.

3) Jamie said, A garbage truck!

d. Look at the first word of the quotation which you underlined. What kind of letter begins the first word in a quotation?

Grammar Guide Review
Begin the first word of a quotation with a **capital letter**.

Add capitalization to the following quotations.

1) Cindy asked, "what is black and white and read (red) all over?"

2) The girls replied, "we don't know."

3) Cindy answered, "a sunburned zebra."

e. Read the following paragraph with your teacher.

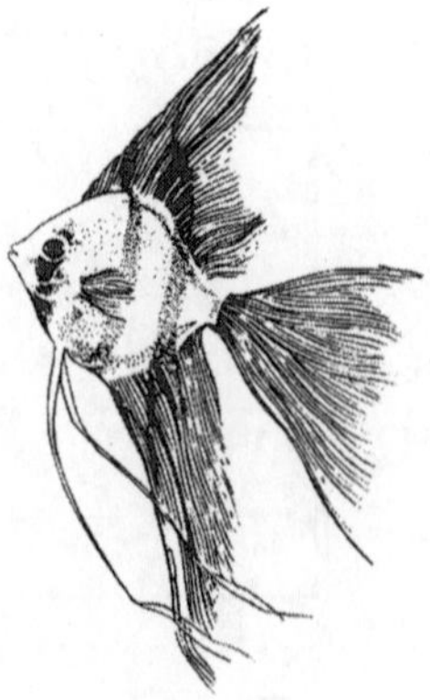

The Tropical Fish Store has many different kinds of sea creatures. They have thirty separate tanks with colorful tropical fish. The fish store has fish of all shapes, sizes, and colors. In the back of the store there are ten tanks with giant lobsters and crabs. The store even sells small octopuses and squid. The Tropical Fish Store also sells supplies and food for all the fish and other creatures they carry. You can buy aquariums and food for the tiniest guppy to the largest lobster.

f. After reading the paragraph with your teacher think about the facts you learned about the Tropical Fish Store. Decide whether or not the following statements are facts (things that are true) or opinions (what someone thinks). Write **F** for Fact or **O** for Opinion on the line in front of each statement.

1) ____ The Tropical Fish Store carries many different kinds of fish.

2) ____ The Tropical Fish Store sells more than just fish.

3) ____ The Tropical Fish Store is a fun place to visit.

4) ____ The fish at the Tropical Fish Store are the prettiest fish in town.

5) ____ The Tropical Fish Store can supply you with food and aquariums for any creature you buy at the store.

Day 5 a. Take the last sentence of the passage from dictation.
Compare your dictation to the passage and make corrections.

b. Discussion with teacher.

c. Enrichment

1) Mrs. Dot wants to find Mr. Dot. Help her go around the square, clockwise, by using the words *north*, *south*, *east*, and *west*.

First, go ____________.

Second, go ____________.

Third, go ____________.

Then go ____________.

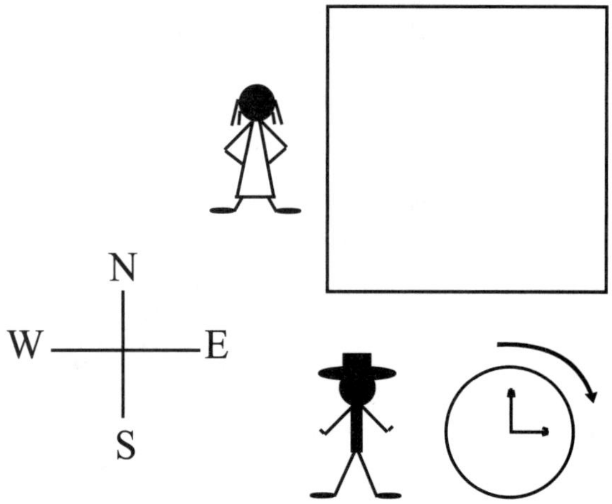

2) Now help Mrs. Dot walk around the same square, counter-clockwise, using the words *north*, *south*, *east*, and *west*.

First, go ____________.

Second, go ____________.

Third, go ____________.

Then go ____________.

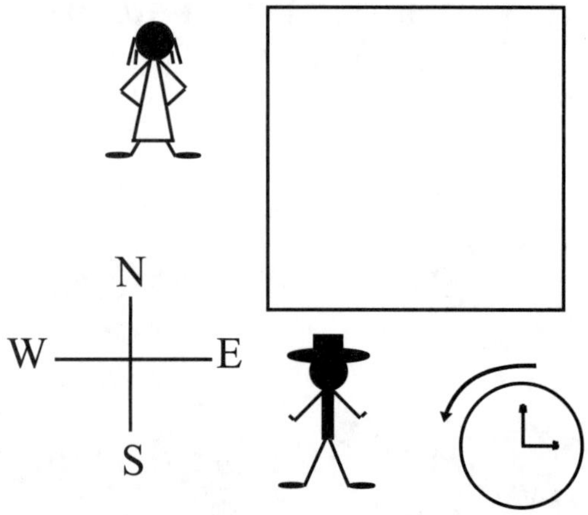

d. Journal Entry:
Ask your parents to help you make a family tree.

e. Handwriting

ad

ed

id

ud

sad

mud

ag

eg

ig

rig

rag

fig

aq

iq

eq

uq

Review Activities

1. Add the suffix **-ed** to these words.

   a. show ____________

   b. lift ____________

   c. pour ____________

   d. look ____________

2. Match the verb on the left to the verb on the right that shows it has already happened.

a. feel	told
b. keep	took
c. pay	kept
d. tell	paid
e. take	felt

3. Underline the actual words spoken.

   Tom said, "I will be late today."

4. Follow the directions.

   a. Write a sentence about yourself stating a fact.

   ____

   ____

   b. Write a sentence about yourself stating an opinion.

   ____

   ____

Assessment 5
(Lessons 19 – 22)

1. Add quotation marks and capitalization.

   I like to play ball said jim.

2. Write the past tense for these verbs. Show that the action has already happened.

   a. play ____________

   b. work ____________

   c. fill ____________

   d. wish ____________

3. Write the past tense for these irregular verbs. Show that the action has already happened.

   a. take ____________

   b. keep ____________

   c. begin ____________

   d. find ____________

4. Write the word *fact* or *opinion* in the blanks.

   a. A statement that tells what someone feels about something is called a(n) ____________.

   b. A statement that tells something true is called a(n) ____________.

5. Add the suffix **–ed** to these words. Next to the word write the sound it makes /**t**/, /**d**/, or /**ed**/.

   a. lift ____________________

   b. jump ____________________

   c. play ____________________

   d. fix ____________________

6. Circle the subject and underline the predicate.

   a. Abi ran after the horse.

   b. The horse jumped the fence.

LITERATURE LINK

Day 1 Listen to your teacher read the vocabulary words.

Vocabulary		
pioneer	Pennsylvania	Squire
Sarah	special	plowing
bareback	tomahawk	respect

Discussion with teacher.

Begin reading the story "Young Daniel – Boy of the Woods."
You will have time tomorrow to finish the story.

Young Daniel – Boy of the Woods

Being part of a pioneer family was exciting. It is true that life was very hard. It is also true that there was always something new happening. Growing up during the 1730s was never dull.

Daniel Boone was born in 1734 in Pennsylvania. The Boone family lived on a farm. His father's name was Squire. His mother's name was Sarah. There were eleven children in the Boone family.

Just like most other pioneer boys Daniel grew up learning many things. His mother wanted him to learn from books, but Daniel wanted to learn the ways of the woods. He always tried to get away when it was time to read or write or spell. He was not very good at these things. He was very good at *other* things.

What Daniel loved to learn most about was the forest, the animals, how to track, and how to hide. These skills would keep him safe. He had a special love for animals. He watched them and learned about them.

Daniel also had to do the work of a pioneer boy. By the time he was ten he chopped wood and helped with the plowing. He helped take care of the animals and hitch the horses. He milked the cows and helped make butter. He helped pick berries when they were ripe and gather nuts before winter came. There was always work to do. The work made Daniel strong.

Daniel learned about Indians, too. He could do many things like the Indians. He could ride a horse bareback (without a saddle). He could throw a tomahawk. He could walk without making a sound. He learned how to get along with Indians, too. They were very proud, and Daniel learned how to treat them with respect.

When Daniel was twelve years old he was given a special present by his father—his first gun! He was so excited! He could hunt like his brothers. Now Daniel was ready to live by himself in the woods. He could take care of himself. Sometimes he would hunt for days or weeks. This was hard for his mother. But soon she understood that Daniel's life would be spent in the forests.

Daniel Boone grew up to be a great man. He helped many people find new places to make their homes. He helped make new roads in the forests. The little pioneer boy from Pennsylvania helped our new country grow. The things Daniel learned about the forests and animals helped us all.

Day 2 a. Finish reading the book or story from yesterday.

b. **Discussion Questions for *The Courage of Sarah Noble*:**

1) Why was Sarah making the journey to New Milford with her father?
2) What was her mother's advice to her as she left?
3) What did the Robinson children tell her about Indians?
4) What book did Sarah bring with her to read?
5) How did Sarah first meet the Indians? Did they become friends?
6) What was Sarah to do while her father went to get the family?
7) How did Sarah like staying with Tall John? What was different for Sarah?
8) How did Sarah feel when her family arrived? How did Sarah feel about herself after they arrived?

Discussion Questions for "Young Daniel – Boy of the Woods":

1) Did Daniel grow up in a big family?
2) Did Daniel like learning things from books? Who wanted him to learn from books?
3) What did Daniel love to learn about? What was his special love?
4) Name some of Daniel's chores.
5) What could Daniel do as well as an Indian?
6) What special gift was Daniel given when he became twelve years old?
7) What did Daniel want to do most of all?
8) How did Daniel's interests as a child help us as a country?

c. After talking with your teacher make a list of five things that pioneer children had to do each day. Include any regular chores you think they did.

d. Now think about what you do each day. Make a list of five things you do each day. Include any regular chores you do.

Compare the two lists. Find things that are the same.

Contrast the two lists. Find things that are different.

e. Now make a list of things you think pioneer children may have done for fun. Look at your list. Are any of their activities things you would like to do today?

f. Talk with your teacher about things you can do around your house to help your family. If you already do chores to help out see if there are any chores you could improve. Together with your teacher make a daily chore list (if you don't have one). Mark every day that you do each chore. Helping makes you feel good about being part of a family.

Day 3 a. With your teacher look at this list of names. Choose one or two names. Use an encyclopedia, library books, or the Internet to read about these people.

Daniel Boone	Davy Crockett
Marcus Whitman	Zebulon Pike
Narcissa Whitman	Lewis and Clark

b. Make a simple timeline of one of the pioneers you read about. Include major events and pictures if you can.

Ex:

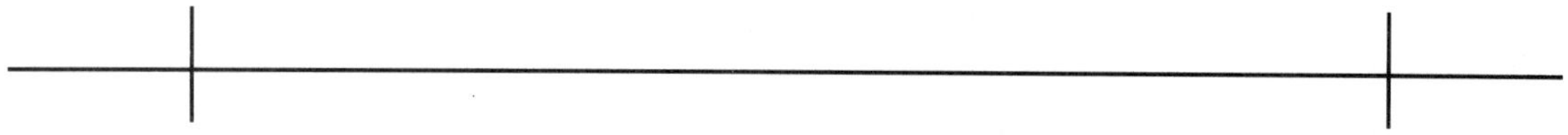

Born 1801 Died 1873

Day 4 After reading about these individuals choose a way to present the information. You may draw a picture or write a paragraph. Prepare for this presentation.

Day 5 a. Look up the words *bravery* and *courage* in the dictionary. Tell your teacher what these two words mean. Write a definition for each word.

b. Discussion with teacher.

c. Talk to your teacher about any of the following characters. Discuss the ways each of them was brave or showed courage.

Queen Esther (Book of Esther)	Joshua (Book of Joshua)
David (as a boy; I Samuel)	Paul (The Apostle)

d. Has there ever been a time in your life when you or someone in your family had to act bravely? Talk with your teacher about this. With your teacher write several sentences telling about what happened and why you think it was brave.

I **C.A.N.** Assessment
Literature Link on *Frontier Life*

After the Literature Link on *Frontier Life* is completed check off each I **C.A.N.** objective with your teacher.

_____	**C**	I can **complete** my work.
_____		I can be **creative**.
_____	**A**	I can be **accurate**.
_____		I can do my work with a good **attitude**.
_____	**N**	I can do my work **neatly**.

EVERYDAY WORDS

All things bright and beautiful,
All creatures, great and small,
All things wise and wonderful,
The Lord God made them all.

"The Creation" by Cecil Frances Alexander

Day 1 a. Write the poem from dictation, or copy it. Compare your copy to the poem and make corrections.

b.

Focus on Spelling
right bright light night might
Bonus Word: wonderful

Copy these spelling words. Say the words aloud as you write them.

c. Enrichment

Fill in the blanks with your spelling words.

1) The opposite of left is

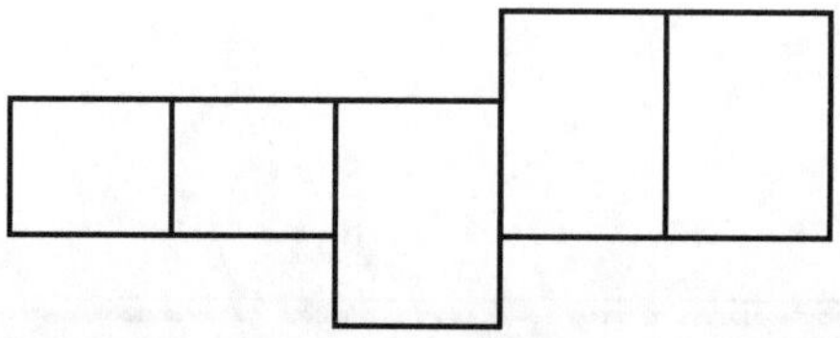

2) The sun is very

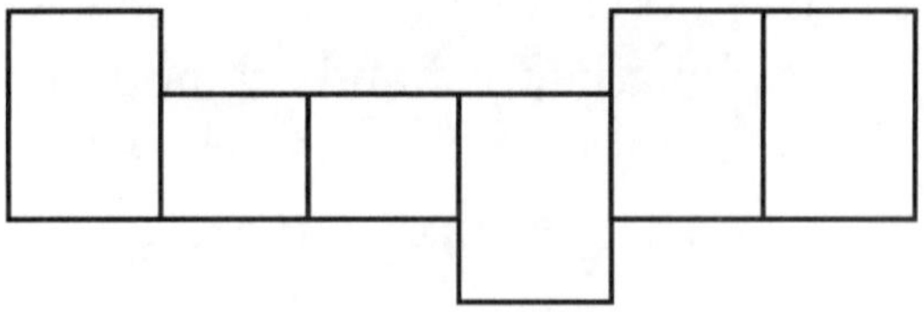

3) The opposite of day is

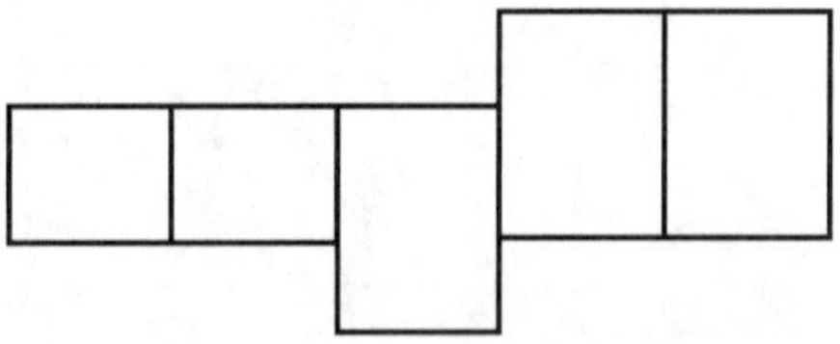

4) Hold on with all your

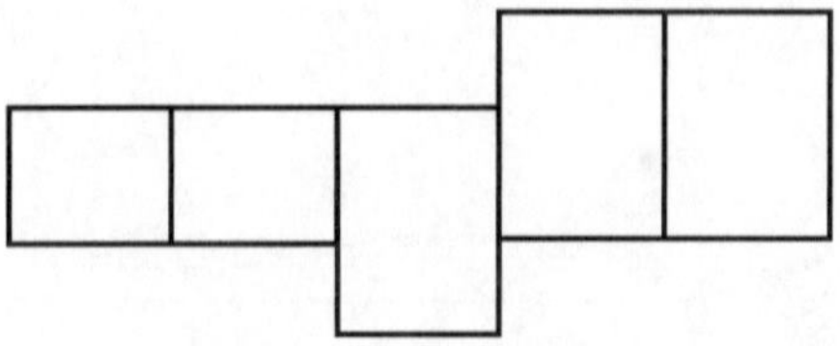

5) The opposite of dark is

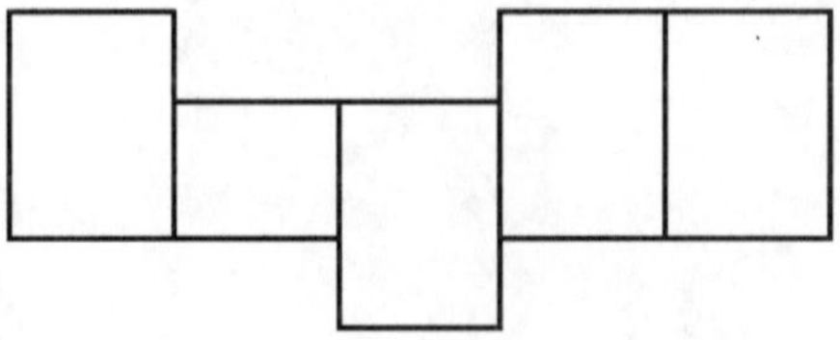

Day 2 a. There are six words in the poem that tell about the things and creatures that God made. Underline each describing word.

Grammar Guide Review
Adjective - a word that describes a person, place, or thing

b. Using a dictionary look up the meanings of the adjectives you underlined. On a separate piece of paper write a brief definition for each adjective.

c. The best way to add a new word to our vocabulary is to use it. Use three pieces of plain white paper and fold them in half. At the top of each section write one of the adjectives you underlined. In each section write the names of people, places, or things that the adjective you wrote at the top could describe. Think of as many examples for each adjective as you can.

Ex: small – child, mouse, insect

d. Choose one word from each section. Make up a sentence using the adjective and the noun it is describing.

Ex: The small mouse ran.

e. **SEE-SPELL-SAY:** Look and **see** each word on the spelling list. **Spell** each word aloud. **Say** the word.

Day 3 a. Using a red crayon or pencil circle the word that has *wonder* as a base, or root, word.

b. Discussion with teacher.

c. Here are some base, or root, words. Add the suffix **-ful** to the end of each word.

1) play ________ 4) joy ________

2) pain ________ 5) color ________

3) thank ________ 6) delight ________

d. Find the word in the passage that has *beauty* as a base, or root, word. When you add the suffix **-ful** to the end of this word the spelling changes. What change was made in the spelling? What rule can you think of that applies to consonant **-y** at the end of a word when adding the suffix **-ful**?

e. Spelling Bee

f. Enrichment

Fill in the blanks using a word that begins with **ch**.

1) I like to play chess and ____________.

2) A little talk is called a ____________.

3) I will __________ the blue one or the red one.

Fill in the blanks using a word that begins with **cr**.

4) The men fish for lobsters and ____________.

5) Dad will fix the __________ on the window.

6) The ants ate the __________ after the picnic.

Day 4 a. Our poem describes things and creatures that the Lord God made. Make a list of your favorite things and creatures.

b. Discussion with teacher.

c. Make up a verse using three of your pictures. Start each line with a capital letter and end it with a comma (,). Add a fourth line that says, *The Lord God made them all.* Start the fourth line with a capital letter and end it with a period. This is called a verse.

d. Spelling Pretest

e. Enrichment

Read the list of words and write the word that comes next.

1) inch foot ____________
2) walk jog ____________
3) cold warm ____________
4) small medium ____________
5) light lighter ____________
6) heavy heavier ____________

Day 5 a. – d. Discussion with teacher.

e. Spelling Test

__________________ __________________

__________________ __________________

__________________ __________________

f. Enrichment

Read the list of words and circle the word that does not rhyme with the other words.

Example: bake take (cook) cake

1)	sing	thing	bring	long
2)	trunk	dunk	mink	sunk
3)	crack	stack	stock	back
4)	sit	bit	slit	mat
5)	sick	kit	lick	tick
6)	lake	truck	sake	bake
7)	pile	while	sail	tile
8)	star	jar	car	mark
9)	long	small	ball	call

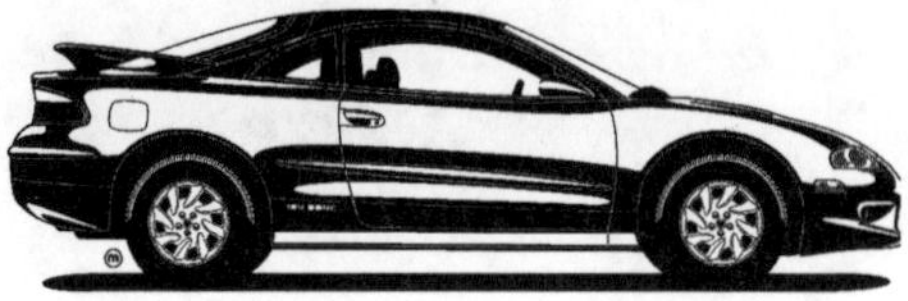

g. Journal Entry: Describe one of your favorite animals.

h. Handwriting: Connecting Letters
When connecting lower case **o** to other letters, the connecting line does not come down to the bottom line. The second letter starts from the middle of the line.

oa

ov

od

ob

og

om

or

oe

ow

of

oh

roast

coat

float

most

soft

Review Activities

1. Think of a describing word, or adjective, that can describe these words.

a. ______________________ tiger c. ______________________ car

b. ______________________ day d. ______________________ girls

2. Add the suffix **-ful** to these words and write the new words.

a. help ______________________ c. rest ______________________

b. hope ______________________ d. joy ______________________

3. Read each sentence. Underline the subject once and underline the predicate twice.

a. Jacob walked to the store.

b. Sarah ran to school today.

c. The dogs like to swim.

d. Mom reads a book every day.

4. Add quotation marks and the correct capitalization to each sentence.

a. I want to go to the movie said Mom.

b. Ryan yelled what time is lunch

c. Dad asked can you help me with this plant

The purple-headed mountain,
The river running by,
The sunset and the morning
That brightens up the sky.

"The Creation" by Cecil Frances Alexander

Day 1 a. Write the poem from dictation or copy it. Compare your copy to the poem and make corrections.

b.

Focus on Spelling

morning evening sunrise sunset sunshine

Bonus Word: Sunday

Copy these spelling words. Say the words aloud as you write them.

c. Enrichment

Unscramble the letters to make your spelling words.

1) sstenu ____________________

2) ringnom ____________________

3) vingeen ____________________

4) isunsre ____________________

5) ssnnieuh ____________________

Day 2 a. Using a red pencil underline only the words that tell the names of things and places in the poem.

b. The word *the* tells us a noun, or naming word, is coming. This is called an article. Circle the word *the* every time you see it in the poem. Read the words you circled to your teacher, then tell her what noun comes after it. The words *a* and *an* are also articles.

Grammar Guide
Article - a small word that tells you a noun is coming *a* *an* *the*

c. In the first line of our poem there are some words between the word *the* and the word *mountain*. Underline these words in blue. These words are adjectives, or words that describe, *mountain*.

d. Read the following sentences to your teacher. Circle the article *the* in each sentence. Underline the noun which comes after the article. Draw an arrow from any adjectives to the noun. Look carefully. There may be more than one article in a sentence.

Ex: The little white dog ran quickly.

1) The fat black cat is playing.

2) Where do you want the new bike?

3) The clock says it's time for lunch.

4) Mother wants the blue plate for the meat.

5) When is the big game?

6) The book I like is on the brown table.

e. **SEE-SPELL-SAY:** Look and **see** each word on the spelling list. **Spell** each word aloud. **Say** the word.

Day 3 a. Discussion with teacher.

b. On a separate piece of paper draw or cut out pictures from a magazine and show what you think these sentences describe. Make more than one picture.

c. On the back of the picture write the sentence from the poem that describes it.

d. Write another sentence on the back of each picture using your own words to describe it.

e. Spelling Bee

f. Enrichment

Fill in the blanks using a word that begins with **wr**.

1) I will ______________________ a letter.

2) He was right, and I was ______________________.

3) I will ______________________ the gift with shiny paper.

Fill in the blanks using a word that begins with **gr**.

4) Dad mows the ______________________.

5) If you are thankful you are ______________________.

6) ______________________ are one of my favorite fruits.

Day 4 a. Practice taking turns reading the parts in this choral reading. After reading it one or two times, trade parts.

Girls or Person 1:	Summer is coming.
Boys or Person 2:	I can't wait!
Girls or Person 1:	It will soon be warm.
Boys or Person 2:	I can't wait!
Girls or Person 1:	Time for swimming.
Boys or Person 2:	I can't wait!
All Together:	Summer is here!

b. – c. Discussion with teacher.

d. Spelling Pretest

________________ ________________

________________ ________________

________________ ________________

e. Enrichment

Put a noun in each blank to make a correct sentence.

1) The ________________ plays.

2) The ________________ works.

3) The ________________ listens.

4) A ________________ gallops.

5) A ________________ chirps.

6) A ________________ buzzes.

Day 5 a. Use the words in the box from Lessons 24 – 25 to fill in the blanks of the crossword puzzle. Remember, one letter to a box. The words either go down or sideways. If a letter is already in a box don't write it again; just go on to the next letter in the word.

bright	mountain	sunset	wonderful
great	river	creatures	morning

DOWN:

1) when the sun goes down

2) all ____________ great and small

3) A large stream is called a ____________.

4) when you wake up

ACROSS:

5) a very tall part of the land

6) all things ____________ and beautiful

7) Something that is very good is ____________.

8) rhymes with *crate*

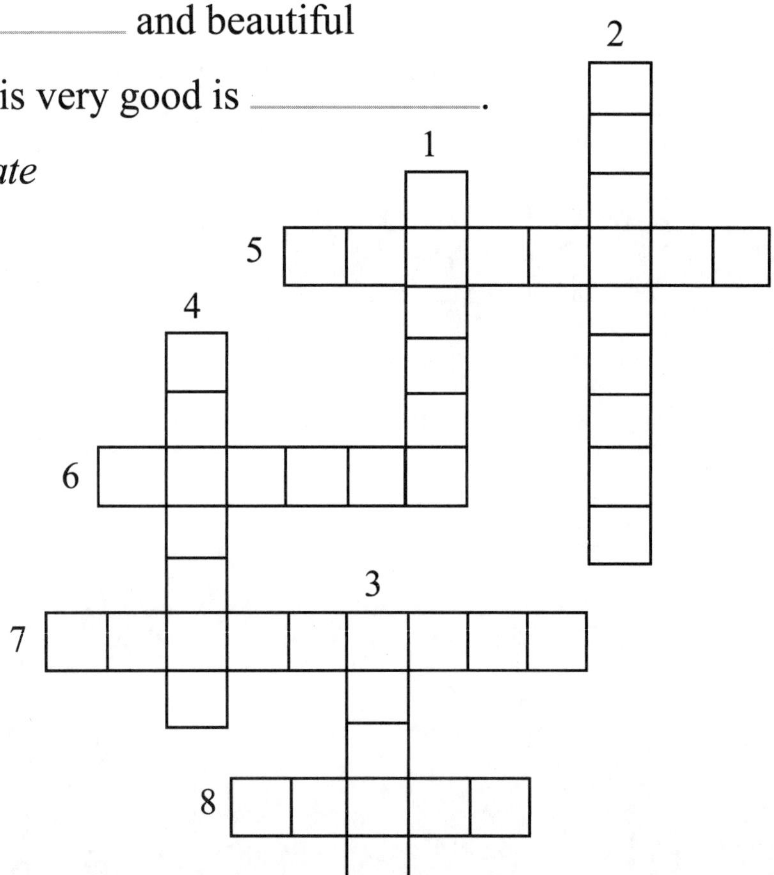

b. Spelling Test

c. Enrichment

Put a verb in each blank to make a complete sentence.

1) My brother ____________________.

2) My sister ____________________.

3) My father ____________________.

4) My friend ____________________.

5) My neighbor ____________________.

6) My mother ____________________.

d. Journal Entry: Describe the scenery near your house.

e. Handwriting: Connecting Letters
When connecting lower case **b** to other letters the connecting line does not come down to the bottom line. The second letter starts from the middle of the line.

be

bw

br

bl

brag

bike

bus

born

ball

black

Review Activities

1. Circle the articles and underline the nouns.

   a. a bear
   b. the horse
   c. an eel
   d. a donkey

2. Underline the nouns. Draw an arrow from the adjective to the noun it describes.

   a. The pretty bird flew away.
   b. The colorful rainbow shone brightly.
   c. The goat ate the old hat.
   d. The dog ran over the pretty flowers.

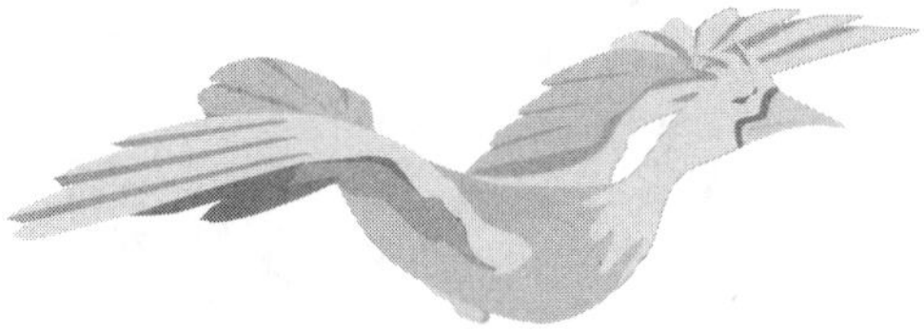

3. Add quotation marks and capitalization to the sentence.

   Sarah asked may I go to the store

   ____

4. Write the past tense for these irregular verbs.

   a. take ____________________
   b. keep ____________________
   c. run ____________________
   d. think ____________________

The cold wind in the winter,
The pleasant summer sun,
The ripe fruits in the garden,
He made them every one.

"The Creation" by Cecil Frances Alexander

Day 1 a. Write the poem from dictation or copy it. Compare your copy to the poem and make corrections.

b.

Focus on Spelling

winter summer spring garden season

Bonus Word: fruit

Copy these spelling words. Say the words aloud as you write them.

c. Enrichment

Fill in each blank with a spelling word.

1) We swim in the ______.

2) The flowers bloom in the ______.

3) Fall is my favorite 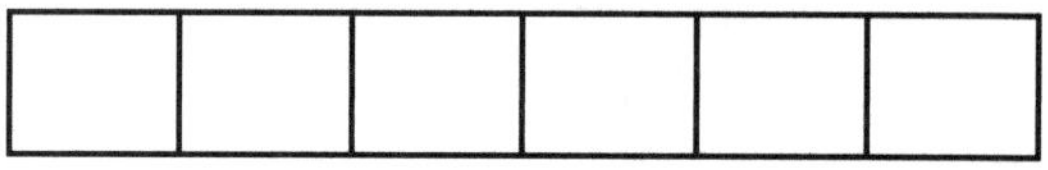 .

4) I wear a coat in the 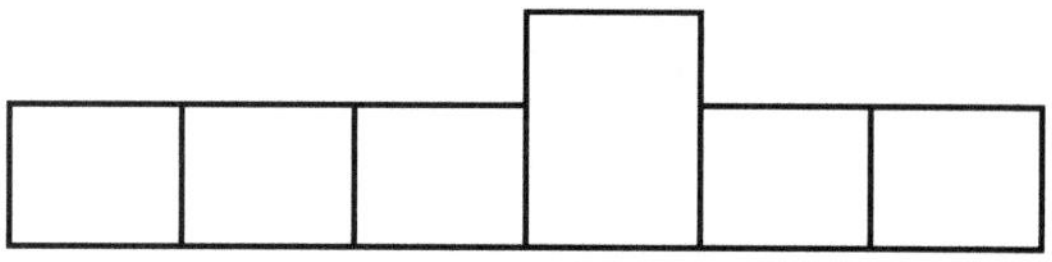 .

5) In the spring we plant our 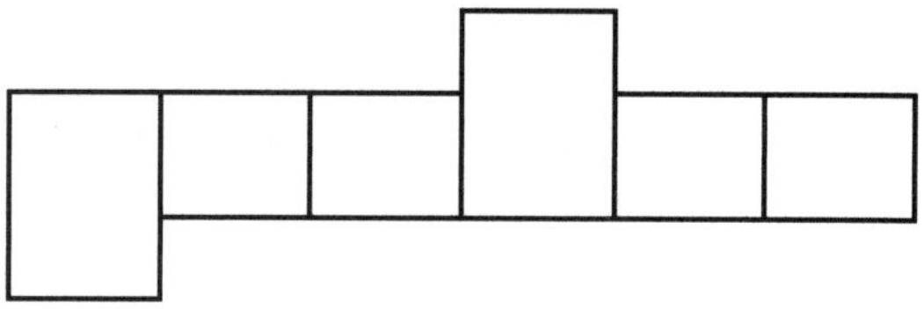 .

Day 2

a. Using a red pencil circle the article *the* every time it appears in our poem. What does the word *the* tell us is coming?

____

b. Using a red pencil underline the nouns, or naming words, that come after the article *the*.

c. Using a blue pencil underline the describing words, or adjectives, that come before several of the nouns.

d. Discussion with teacher.

e. **SEE-SPELL-SAY:** Look and **see** each word on the spelling list. **Spell** each word aloud. **Say** the word.

f. Enrichment

Fill in the blanks using a word that begins with **kn**.

1) I will tie a ____________________.

2) My sister likes to sew and ____________________.

3) I hear a ____________________ on the door.

Fill in the blanks using a word that begins with **fl**.

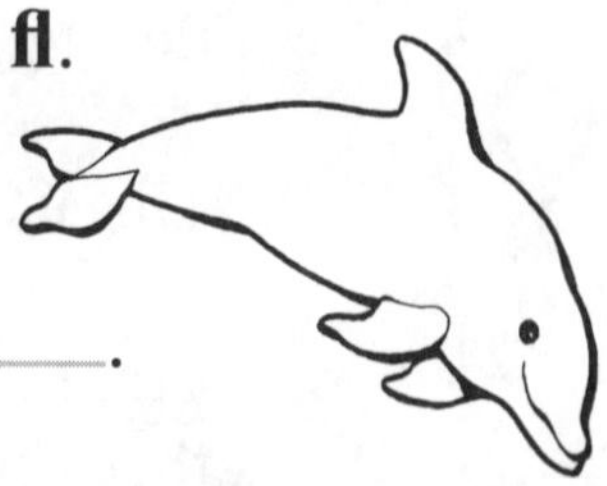

4) The bird ______________________ away.

5) The land has no hills; it is ______________________.

6) The dolphin waved his ______________________.

Fill in the blanks using a word that begins with **qu**.

7) The king and ______________________ sat on the thrones.

8) Two pints equal one ______________________.

9) A turtle is slow, and a rabbit is ______________________.

Day 3

a. When you are counting syllables in a word clap each time you hear a part of the word. Here are some examples:

car/pet – 2 claps hap/py – 2 claps
hot – 1 clap won/der/ful – 3 claps

b. Draw a line between the two syllables of each of these words:

1) winter 3) summer 5) garden

2) purple 4) sunset 6) running

c. Draw lines to show where to divide each syllable. Remember your rule about where to divide syllables.

1) afternoon 2) tomorrow 3) understood 4) yesterday

d. Read each word. Write 1, 2, or 3 on the line to show how many syllables are in each word:

1) __________ river 6) __________ morning

2) __________ sky 7) __________ wonderful

3) __________ beautiful 8) __________ small

4) __________ mountain 9) __________ headed

5) __________ great 10) __________ bright

e. Spelling Bee

Day 4 a. – b. Discussion with teacher.

c. Create a picture or two for this verse to go with the picture you have for the other verses.

d. Discussion with teacher.

e. Spelling Pretest

______________________ ______________________

______________________ ______________________

______________________ ______________________

f. Enrichment

Write an adjective, or describing word, for each noun.

Ex: happy boy

1) ______________ flower

2) ______________ fish

3) ______________ lunch

4) ______________ boy

5) ______________ girl

6) ______________ man

7) ______________ house

8) ______________ boat

9) ______________ tree

Day 5 a. – b. Discussion with teacher.

c. Spelling Test

d. Journal Entry: What is your favorite time of year? Explain why.

e. Handwriting: Connecting Letters
When connecting lower case **w** to other letters, the connecting line does not come down to the bottom line. The second letter starts from the middle of the line.

wa

we

wu

wi

wh

wo

wl

wags

will

what

paws

went

won't

warm

Review Activities

1. Write 1, 2, or 3 to show the number of syllables in each word. Draw lines to show where to divide each syllable.

a. library
b. dinosaur
c. survival
d. potato

2. Fill in each blank with an adjective.

a. We watched the ________________________ sunset.
b. The ____________________ wind blew through the trees.
c. John walked the ___________________ dogs.
d. Where is the _____________________ crayon?

3. Rewrite the sentences replacing the nouns with the correct pronoun.

a. *Sarah and Eric* liked the book.

____

b. *Sarah, Eric, and I* ate dinner at my house.

____

c. *Travis* ran in the race on Tuesday.

____

4. Read each sentence. Underline the subject once and underline the predicate twice.

a. Sarah likes horses.
b. Tim buys milk every day.
c. Our hamsters run all around the house.
d. Dad cooks every Friday.

He gave us eyes to see them,
And lips that we might tell
How great is God Almighty,
Who has made all things well!

"The Creation" by Cecil Frances Alexander

Day 1 a. Write the poem from dictation, or copy it. Compare your copy to the poem and make corrections.

b.

Focus on Spelling

head dead bread instead ready

Bonus Word: pleasant

Copy these spelling words. Say the words aloud as you write them.

c. Enrichment

Fill in the blanks to make your spelling words.

1)

	e	a	

2)

		e	a	

3) 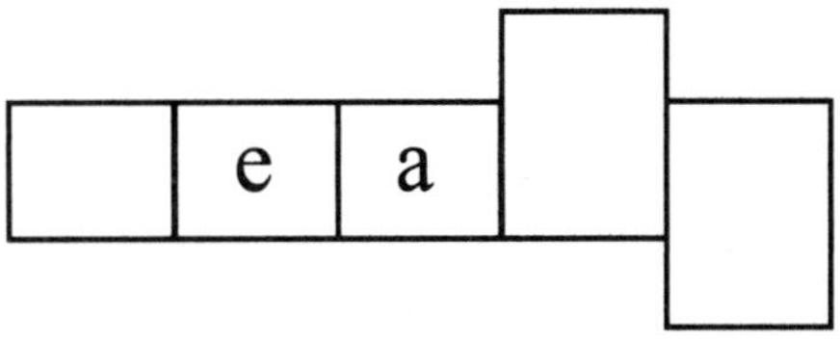

4) 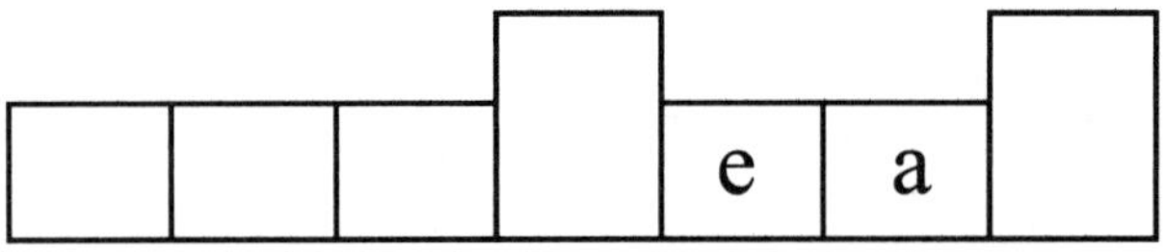

5) 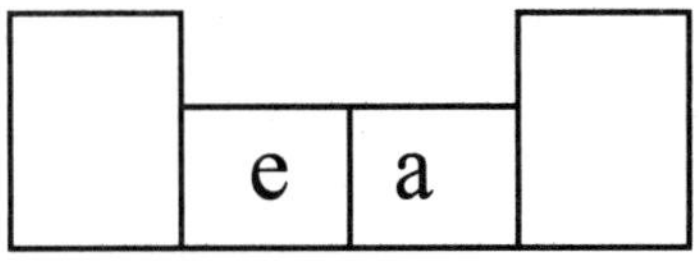

Day 2 a. In the last line of the verse there is a word that tells us how God Almighty made all things. Underline this word.

Grammar Guide
Adverb - a word that describes a verb, and adjective, or another adverb

b. Here is a correct sentence: That was a good dinner.

Good describes *dinner*. *Dinner* is a thing.

Is this sentence correct?

He plays ball good.

Plays is a doing word, so use *well*. *Well* tells how the playing was done.

He plays ball well. This sentence is correct.

c. Read each sentence. Choose the word *good* or *well* to write in each blank.

1) We had a ________________ time at the park.

2) This cookie is very ________________.

3) The team played ________________ today.

4) She painted that picture very ________________.

5) My dad is a ________________ fisherman.

6) Our fishing trip went ________________.

d. **SEE-SPELL-SAY:** Look and **see** each word on the spelling list. **Spell** each word aloud. **Say** the word.

e. Enrichment

Look at the diagram below and answer the questions.

1) What letters are in the square? ________________

2) What letters are **only** in the square? ________________

3) What letters are in the circle? ________________

4) What letters are **only** in the circle? ________________

5) What letters are in both the circle and the square? ________________

6) What letters are outside the circle and square? ________________

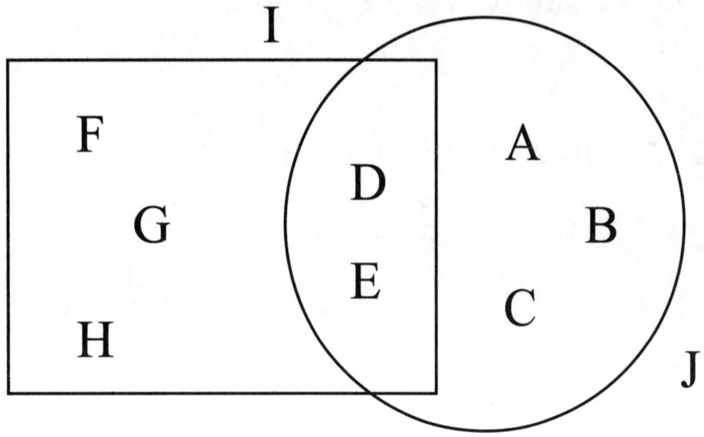

Day 3 a. You are going to find synonyms, words that mean about the same thing, for each word. Look up each word in a thesaurus and write a list of synonyms for it. The words in a thesaurus are in alphabetical order like a dictionary.

1) beautiful ________________

2) great ________________

3) wise ________________

4) good ________________

5) wonderful ____________________

6) small ____________________

Tell your teacher a sentence using one of the synonyms you found for each word.

b. Read each sentence. Replace the italicized word with a synonym that you think fits best.

1) Mother's new dress is *beautiful.*

____

2) The king was a very *great* man.

____

3) I don't think it is *wise* to play near the street.

____

4) The sunny weather is *good.*

____

5) Getting to see the mountains was *wonderful.*

____

6) The new puppies are very *small.*

____

c. Spelling Bee

d. Enrichment

On a separate sheet of paper, write your name, allowing a column for each letter of your name. Underneath each letter think of as many foods as you can that begin with that letter, and write them down.

Ex:

S	A	M
spaghetti	apple	marshmallow

Day 4 a. – b. Discussion with teacher. Use the space provided on pages 270 and 271 for the following activity.

c. Make a list of several things that God made as described in Genesis 1. Remember to number your list and to put a period after each number. Place each item on your list in the column of the day in which it was created.

d. Why didn't we have a Day 7 on our chart? What did God do on the seventh day of Creation? ______________________________

e. Spelling Pretest

______________________ ______________________

______________________ ______________________

______________________ ______________________

Day 5 a. – c. Discussion with teacher.

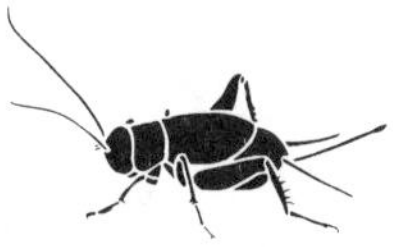

d. Spelling Test

______________________ ______________________

______________________ ______________________

______________________ ______________________

e. Enrichment

Each word represents a whole. List three things that are a part of the whole.

Ex: body - Possible answers: head, arm, legs

1) insect ______________________________

2) door ______________________________

3) computer ______________________________

4) mouse ______________________________

5) house ______________________________

6) family ______________________________

f. Journal Entry: Describe a typical day at your house.

Day 1	**Day 2**	**Day 3**

Day 4	Day 5	Day 6

g. Handwriting: Connecting Letters
When connecting lower case **v** to other letters, the connecting line does not come down to the bottom line. The second letter starts from the middle of the line.

va

ve

vu

vi

vh

vo

vl

van

oven

invite

vest

over

wave

Review Activities

1. Write the word *good* or *well* to complete these sentences.

   a. I played ________________ at my baseball game.

   b. Have you been feeling ________________?

   c. How ________________ do you know Jim?

   d. The cake tastes ________________.

2. Match the words on the left to a synonym on the right.

a. careful	weary
b. breezy	frightened
c. afraid	simple
d. tired	cautious
e. plain	windy

3. Write an adjective to describe each noun.

   a. house ________________

   b. chair ________________

   c. horse ________________

   d. car ________________

4. Read each sentence and decide which needs an apostrophe. Write the apostrophe.

   a. The cats like to play.

   b. We need to get the cats food.

   c. These are the girls presents.

   d. We saw the girls at the park.

thesaurus [thi-sawr-us] noun

A book of synonyms and antonyms
plural: thesauruses, thesauri

synonyms:
reference book
glossary
lexicon
onomasticon

Day 1

a. Discussion with teacher.

b. Review synonyms in Lesson 2 and antonyms in Lesson 10.

c. This is how the word large would appear in a thesaurus:

large [lahrj] adjective
a size greater than average of its kind
He was hungry, so he ordered the large pizza.
synonyms: big, enormous, grand, hefty, massive
antonyms: little, shrimpish, small, undersized

d. Review alphabetical order in Lesson 5.

e. Put the following words in alphabetical order. Copy two synonyms for each word.

gentle delicious book funny

f. Enrichment

You are going on vacation. It is time to pack your suitcase. Think of something you can put in your suitcase using each letter of the word *suitcase*. Write as many things as you can.

Ex: S – sweater, U – underwear, etc.

S ____________________

U ____________________

I ____________________

T ____________________

C ____________________

A ____________________

S ____________________

E ____________________

Day 2 a. Read the following sentence:

We watched the man **walk** down the street.

In your thesaurus, find three synonyms for the word *walk*. Replace the word *walk* with each of the three synonyms. How does the sentence change as you use each synonym?

______________ ______________ ______________

b. Read this sentence:

We had a **good** day.

Find three synonyms for the word *good*. Replace the word good with one each of the synonyms.

______________ ______________ ______________

c. Put the following words in alphabetical order and write synonyms for each.

family fly forest fake

____

____

____

____

d. Put the following words in alphabetical order:

darling deep dull delightful drop drip dark

____

____

____

____

____

____

____

Day 3 a. Using your thesaurus, replace the italicized words in this passage from *The Jungle Book* by Rudyard Kipling with synonyms:

Father Wolf taught the meaning of things in the jungle till every *rustle* ____________ in the grass, every breath of the *warm* ______________ night air, every note of the owls, every *scratch* ____________ of a bat's claws as it *roosted* ____________ for a while in a tree, and every splash of every *little* ______________fish jumping in a pool meant just as much to him as the *work* ______________ of his office means to a business man. When he was not learning he *sat* ___________ out in the sun and *slept* ______________, and *ate* ______________ and went to sleep again. When he felt *dirty* ___________ or *hot* ___________ he *swam* _____________ in the forest pools.

b. Replace the words with different synonyms. Does the meaning change?

Father Wolf taught the meaning of things in the jungle till every *rustle* ____________ in the grass, every breath of the *warm* ________________ night air, every note of the owls, every *scratch* ______________ of a bat's claws as it *roosted* _____________ for a while in a tree, and every splash of every *little* _______________fish jumping in a pool meant just as much to him as the *work* _______________ of his office means to a business man. When he was not learning he *sat* ___________ out in the sun and *slept* _______________, and *ate* _______________ and went to sleep again. When he felt *dirty* ____________ or *hot* ____________ he *swam* ______________ in the forest pools.

c. Put the synonyms you chose in the first exercise in alphabetical order.

____________________ ____________________

____________________ ____________________

____________________ ____________________

____________________ ____________________

____________________ ____________________

____________________ ____________________

Day 4 a. Find two synonyms and two antonyms for each of these words:

	synonyms	antonyms
laugh	____________________	____________________
love	____________________	____________________
yell	____________________	____________________

b. Write a sentence for each word. Then rewrite the sentences replacing the word with a synonym. Finally, rewrite each sentence, replacing the word with an antonym.

Ex: It was a **sunny** day.
It was a **bright** day. (synonym)
It was a **dark** day. (antonym)

____

____

____

____

____

____

____

____

____

c. Using your thesaurus, replace the italicized words in this passage from *Pollyanna* by Eleanor H. Porter with antonyms

The *little* ___________room was *cooler* __________now, and the air blew in *fresh* _____________ and *sweet* _____________. Outside the birds were twittering *joyously* _____________, and Pollyanna *flew* _____________ to the window to listen to them.

d. Enrichment

Fill in the blanks using a word that begins with **pr**.

1) The church ________________ for the sick.

2) The needle ________________ my finger.

3) The ________________ was $2.00.

Fill in the blanks using a word that begins with **bl**.

4) I will keep my eyes open and not ________________.

5) The baby plays with her building ________________.

6) The old photograph was in ________________ and white.

Day 5. a. Spell the words for your teacher.

b. Writing from Dictation

1)

2)

c. Discussion with teacher.

1)

2)

d. Enrichment

Write an adjective, or describing word, for each noun.

1) ______ mountain

2) ______ sunset

3) ______ rainbow

4) ______ rain

5) ______ snow

6) ______ clouds

e. Journal Entry: Make a list of people you talk to on the telephone. Describe your last conversation with someone on your list.

f. Handwriting

oats

boat

wait

vest

over

bowl

west

very

old

best

when

van

ox

brave

vote

word

only

wave

Review Activities

Choose the skills your student needs

1. Put these words in alphabetical order:

   a. tiger, blossom, joke, pitcher

   b. acorn, August, Apple, ate

   c. crinkle, cry, crackle, crush

Use a thesaurus to complete the following exercises.

2. Replace the italicized words in this sentence from *The Tale of Peter Rabbit* by Bearix Potter with a synonym.

Peter got down very *quietly* ______________ off the wheelbarrow and started *running* ______________ as *fast* ______________ as he could go, along a *straight* _________walk behind some black-currant bushes.

3. Replace the italicized words with an antonym.

Peter got down very *quietly* ______________ off the wheelbarrow and started *running* ______________ as *fast* ______________ as he could go, along a *straight* _________walk behind some black-currant bushes.

4. Write a contraction for each pair of words.

   a. do not ____________________

   b. cannot ____________________

   c. should not ____________________

   d. he will ____________________

Assessment 6

(Lessons 24 - 28)

1. Add adjectives, or describing words, to these sentences.

   a. Noah rode his ____________________ bike.

   b. He beeped his ____________________ horn.

   c. It made a ____________________ noise.

   d. Noah is a ____________________ boy.

2. Add the suffix **-ful** to these words.

   a. play ____________________

   b. care ____________________

   c. thought ____________________

   d. rest ____________________

3. Circle the articles and underline the nouns.

   a. A child fell into the water.

   b. The boy laughed at the clown.

   c. A lion roared at the crowd.

4. Underline the nouns and draw an arrow from the adjective to the noun it describes.

   The tall man was walking his gray dog.

5. Write the contractions.

   a. I am ____________________

   b. does not ____________________

   c. let us ____________________

   d. have not ____________________

6. Put the following words in alphabetical order:

   ask teach calmly important beautiful

7. Using a thesaurus, find two synonyms and two antonyms for each of the words.

EVERYDAY WORDS

"Please, Etty, listen. I realize it must be difficult for you. But the point is, it's going to be a very bad flood. You have to leave the trolley. You can't stay here. You must move to higher ground," said Jeremy.

Day 1 a. Write the literature passage from dictation, or copy it. Compare your copy to the literature passage and make corrections.

b.

Focus on Spelling

noise spoil point coin boil

Bonus Word: difficult

Copy these spelling words. Say the words aloud as you write them.

c. Enrichment

Fill in the blanks to make your spelling words.

1) [ ] o i [ ]

2) [ ] o i [ ] [ ]

3) [ ] [ ] o i [ ]

4) [ ] o i [ ] [ ]

5) [ ] o i [ ]

Day 2 a. Read the literature passage silently to yourself. Who is speaking?

____

b. With a blue pencil underline the words Jeremy spoke.

c. What punctuation mark shows you what Jeremy said? __________

d. Now read the literature passage aloud to your teacher. Try to read the words Jeremy spoke as he would have spoken them.

e. How many sentences did Jeremy speak? __________

f. How could you tell when a new sentence began? __________

____

g. Although Jeremy spoke several sentences they are all part of what he said. A quotation mark is placed before his first spoken word and after his last spoken word.

h. This quotation ends with a comma. The comma is inside the closing quotation mark followed by *said Jeremy*.

Add quotation marks and commas in the following sentences. Remember to place the comma before the closing quotation mark.

1) Let's plant a garden said Rachel.

2) Yes, we can grow tomatoes said Jake.

3) I want to water the garden said Emily.

i. Complete the following quotation with something you might say.

"____

__________________________," said ________________________.

(*student's name*)

j. Try writing your own quotation.

____

____

k. **SEE-SPELL-SAY:** Look and **see** each word on the spelling list. **Spell** each word aloud. **Say** the word.

Day 3

a. Find the two contractions in our literature passage and underline them.

b. Look at the words that go together to make contractions. What letters were taken out?

let us – let's __________ does not – doesn't __________

c. Match the following words with their contractions:

can not	didn't
I am	it's
did not	can't
it is	I'll
I will	don't
do not	I'm

d. Use the contractions from **3c** in these sentence blanks:

1) (*I am*) ____________________ going out to play.

2) Bob (*can not*) ____________________ go fishing now.

3) We (*did not*) ____________________ see the puppies.

4) (*I will*) ____________________ get the bat and ball.

5) (*It is*) ____________________ time to feed the puppies.

6) We (*do not*) ____________________ have time to play ball.

e. Spelling Bee

Day 4 a. From reading the literature passage we can tell there is going to be a flood. Look up the word *flood* in the dictionary. Discuss what a flood is with your teacher.

b. Look up the word *warn* or *warning* in the dictionary. Discuss its meaning with your teacher.

c. Discussion with teacher.

d. Write a paragraph of three or four sentences about the warning you received. Use complete sentences to answer the following questions.

1) What were you warned about?
2) Did you listen to the warning?
3) What did or did not happen?
4) How did you feel after it was over?

____

____

____

____

____

____

____

e. Spelling Pretest

______________________ ______________________

______________________ ______________________

______________________ ______________________

Day 5 a. Listen to your teacher as she reads the vocabulary words. Read aloud the story, "Katie's Day at the Vet's Office."

Vocabulary					
veterinary	vet	kennel	unusual	monkeys	raccoons
squirrels	lizards	supplies	leashes	newspapers	
recycle	laundry	towels	groomer	finish	x-rays

Katie's Day at the Vet's Office

by Katie Bennett

One or two days a week I help at the veterinary office. I ride my bike there because it is so close to our house. I really like working with animals. When I get there I have a list of things I need to do. Before I start on my list I walk around the kennels and see what kinds of animals are staying there. Usually there are just dogs, cats, and birds. Sometimes there are unusual animals like monkeys, raccoons, squirrels, and lizards.

Now it is time to start my list. My first job is to refill supplies. There are bags and leashes to put out and bottles to refill. Next I am off to sort and stack newspapers. They don't like to use the shiny ads in the cages. I take them out to the recycle bin and stack the papers in a neat pile. Another thing that I have to do is the laundry.

Some of the cats and dogs that stay there have blankets or towels in their kennels.

My favorite part is doing things with the animals. I have to help clean the cages and walk the dogs. The cats all get clean newspaper. Then I get to help the groomer. I wash a dog while she trims and brushes a different dog or cat. We wash the dogs in a regular bathtub that is up high so we don't have to bend over.

That is about everything on my list I have to do. When I finish my list I walk around to see if anyone needs help. Sometimes I get to help the veterinarian. Usually he has me hold the animals while he looks at it. Other times I take the lunch order, file papers and x-rays, or clean up.

When I get tired of working I ride my bike home. I always have fun working at the vet's office.

(Katie Bennett is a former homeschool student from Indialantic, FL.)

b. **Discussion Questions**

1) What does a veterinarian, or vet, do? Why does Katie help at the vet's office?
2) What kinds of animals are usually at the vet's office? What different kinds of animals are there sometimes?
3) What are some of the jobs Katie has to do before she works with the animals?
4) Why does Katie wash blankets and towels at the vet's office?
5) What does Katie do with the dogs? What does she do with the cats?
6) How does Katie help the vet?
7) Does Katie like working at the vet's office? Would you like to help at the vet's office?
8) What things do you think Katie is learning by helping at the vet's office?

c. Spelling Test

d. Enrichment

Josh is taller than Mike. Mike is taller than Steve. Label the pictures of the boys.

e. Journal Entry: Describe one of your trips to a doctor or dentist.

f. Handwriting

As

An

All

Am

Come

Call

Cub

City

1 2 Only

Oats

Olive

Over

1
2
Quick

Queen

Quit

Question

Review Activities

1. Add quotation marks.

   Jessie asked, May I have a cookie?

2. What words do these contractions replace?

   a. I'll ______________________

   b. don't ______________________

   c. can't ______________________

   d. it's ______________________

3. How do you begin every sentence?

   ____

4. How do you begin every paragraph?

   ____

5. Match the vocabulary word with the correct meaning.

a. veterinarian	to complete a task
b. unusual	a doctor for animals
c. finish	a group of clothing being washed
d. laundry	different from the ordinary

Notes

Lesson 30 — Everyday Words

The little black moorhen strutted here and there, poking into this and that. In the end, she turned to Jeremy and said, "Oh, I don't know. Let the flood take it all. I'll make a new nest when I come back."

Day 1 a. Write the literature passage from dictation, or copy it. Compare your copy to the model and make corrections.

b.

Focus on Spelling

new glue tool soup flew

Bonus Word: juice

Copy these spelling words. Say the words aloud as you write them.

c. Enrichment

Find your spelling words in the puzzle: new glue flew tool soup

w	m	f	r	o	m	b
i	n	e	w	g	e	s
t	o	q	g	l	t	o
o	t	w	a	u	o	u
o	e	f	l	e	w	p
l	r	o	n	m	v	g

Day 2 a. Underline the contractions in our literature passage.

b. Cross out the letters you will leave out to make these contractions.
Ex: she ~~i~~s – she's

1) I am – I'm
2) we are – we're
3) is not – isn't
4) does not – doesn't
5) do not – don't
6) you are – you're
7) was not – wasn't
8) we will – we'll
9) I have – I've
10) are not – aren't

c. Write the correct contraction in each blank:

1) (*I have*) ____________ washed my shirt.
2) We (*are not*) ____________ going to the store.
3) Mother will make a snack when (*we are*) ____________ done.
4) She (*is not*) ____________ on my soccer team.
5) The dog (*does not*) ____________ wear its collar.
6) Dad said (*you are*) ____________ going to the game.
7) Bob said (*we will*) ____________ be in the play.
8) This (*was not*) ____________ the book I wanted to read.

d. Read the exact words the moorhen said just as she would have spoken them.

e. How did you know which words were the moorhen's words?

---

f. **SEE-SPELL-SAY:** Look and **see** each word on the spelling list. **Spell** each word aloud. **Say** the word.

Day 3 a. The literature passage tells about some new kinds of animals. Look up the word *vole* in an encyclopedia or on the Internet.

1) Where do these animals usually live?
2) What do they look like?

b. Look up *moorhen.* Answer the same questions in **3a**.

c. List the facts you find.

vole	**moorhen**

d. Look at your lists of facts. Compare the lists by finding one or two facts that are the same about each creature. Contrast the lists by finding one or two facts that are different. Point these out to your teacher.

e. Spelling Bee

Day 4 a. The letters **le** at the end of a word usually says /**l**/.

Ex: apple candle

Find the word in our literature passage that ends in **-le**. Write the word and underline **-le**.

____

b. The letters **el** at the end of the word can also say /**l**/.

Write these words and underline the two letters that make the /**l**/ sound:

shovel travel

____________________ ____________________

c. The letters **al** at the end of the word can also say /**l**/.

Write these words and underline the two letters that make the /**l**/ sound:

petal final

____________________ ____________________

Phonics Fact

The letters **-le**, **-el**, and **-al** at the end of a word say /**l**/.

d. Write each word in the category that shows the correct /l/ sound.

middle	metal	bottle	circle	handle
nickel	castle	animal	oval	final
battle	squirrel	uncle	travel	petal
people	shovel	table	settle	several

-le	-el	-al

e. Spelling Pretest

f. Enrichment

Jill is shorter than Lizzie. Lizzie is shorter than Amy.
Label the pictures of the girls.

______________ ______________ ______________

Day 5 a. Read the literature passage aloud to your teacher. How does the moorhen seem to be acting? What do you think she is feeling?

b. Try to find the two phrases in the first sentence that show you the moorhen is worried and upset.

____

____

c. Read this sentence for your teacher:

When we went into the store Mom looked at this and that.

What did Mom look at in the store? ______________

Do we know from this sentence exactly what she looked at? ______________

d. These expressions "here and there" and "this and that" show a decision has not yet been made. In the sentence above it shows that Mom hadn't really looked at anything specifically. Make up at least one sentence using each expression.

e. Spelling Test

f. Enrichment

Read each list of words and circle the word that does not rhyme with the other words.

1) tear oar core soar
2) king back wing thing
3) jog log cog gas
4) chew chin flew clue
5) with write kite flight
6) corn born torn cork
7) flock home dome foam
8) sock rock dock tick
9) rip hot not pot

g. Journal Entry: Pretend you can fly for one day.
Describe the day and the things you would see during the day.

h. Handwriting

Hi

Hello

Hat

Hot

Hurry

1 2 3

Mom

Make

Most

Meal

Mix

1 2 3

Nate

Near

No

Night

Nurse

Review Activities

1. Write the correct contraction in each blank.

   a. I hope (*you are*) ________________ coming.

   b. (*We are*) ________________ going on vacation.

   c. I (*have not*) ________________ seen my grandma in a long time.

   d. She (*does not*) ________________ know we are coming.

2. Circle the word spelled incorrectly in each group.

a.	castle	middle	people	shovle
b.	travel	squirrel	tabel	nickel
c.	final	battal	animal	oval

3. Fill in the blank with an adjective to describe the noun.

   a. We rode in a ________________ car.

   b. Noah has a ________________ horse.

   c. We found ________________ shells at the beach.

   d. Dad bought us a ________________ ball.

4. Add the suffix **-ed** to each word. Read the new word.

   a. hope ________________

   b. look ________________

   c. pick ________________

   d. blame ________________

The moorhen's thanks gave Jeremy a warm feeling as he continued on his way. "Finally," he thought to himself, "someone finally listened to me. Someone believed."

Day 1 a. Write the literature passage from dictation, or copy it. Compare your copy to the model and make corrections.

b.

Focus on Spelling

chief believe field piece yield

Bonus Word: finally

Copy these spelling words. Say the words aloud as you write them.

c. Enrichment

Fill in the blanks to make your spelling words.

1) ___ i e ___ ___

2) ___ i e ___ ___

3) ___ ___ ___ i e ___ ___

4) ___ i e ___ ___

5) ___ ___ i e ___

Day 2 a. Quotation marks (“ ”) are used to show Jeremy’s thoughts. Circle the quotation marks.

b. Underline *only* Jeremy’s thoughts.

c. Ask your teacher this question:

“What will we do after this lesson?”

Now write down her answer. Place a comma after her last word. Place quotation marks around all the words which were spoken. Be sure to place the closing quotation mark after the comma. Next to the closing quotation mark write *said the teacher*. Place a period at the end of the sentence.

Ex: "We will have a snack," said the teacher.

____

____

____

Now ask your teacher to read this question to you:

"What is your favorite snack?"

Write down your answer using quotation marks.

Ex: "My favorite snack is raisins," said (*your name*).

____

____

____

____

d. **SEE-SPELL-SAY:** Look and **see** each word on the spelling list. **Spell** each word aloud. **Say** the word.

e. Enrichment

Fill in the blanks using a word that begins with **fr**.

1) This is to you ____________________ me.

2) Josh is my best ____________________.

3) We eat ____________________ vegetables from our garden.

Fill in the blanks using a word that begins with **gl**.

4) I will pour a ____________________ of milk.

5) I am not sad; I am ____________________.

6) The stars sparkle and ____________________.

Day 3 a. Make a list of the three words from the literature passage that end with **-ed**.

_______________ _______________

_______________ _______________

b. Draw a line between the suffix **-ed** and the base word on all three words:

Ex: lik/ed jump/ed

c. Are all the base words spelled correctly without the suffix?

____

d. Add **-ed** to each of these words:

1) love _______________ 5) bake _______________

2) show _______________ 6) pass _______________

3) talk _______________ 7) play _______________

4) please _______________ 8) name _______________

e. Let's review how you show something has already happened. (Past tense)

1) Most words just add the suffix **-ed**.
2) Short words ending in a short vowel and a consonant double the last consonant before adding **-ed**.
3) Words ending in a silent **e** drop the **e** before adding **-ed**.
4) Words ending in a consonant and **y** change the **y** to **i** before adding **-ed**.
5) Words ending in a vowel and **y** just add **-ed**.
6) Some words (irregular words) change their spelling completely.

Write a word to fill each blank:

1) Today, I *walk*. Yesterday, I ______________________.

2) Today, I *hop*. Yesterday, I ______________________.

3) Today, I *like*. Yesterday, I ______________________.

4) Today, I *hurry*. Yesterday, I ______________________.

5) Today, I *pray*. Yesterday, I ______________________.

6) Today, I *tell*. Yesterday, I ______________________.

f. Spelling Bee

Day 4 a. The sound /**er**/ is spelled several ways. The most common way this sound is spelled is **er**, **ir**, and **ur**.

driver	later
sir	third
burn	nurse

Underline the two letters in each word that spell the /**er**/ sound.

b. Another way to spell the /**er**/ sound is with the letters **-ar** at the end of the word, like this:

dollar cellar

Underline the two letters in each word that spell the /**er**/ sound.

c. A third way to spell the /**er**/ sound is with the letters **-or** at the end of the word, like this:

color doctor

Underline the two letters in each word that spell the /**er**/ sound.

d. Write each word in the category that shows how the /**er**/ sound is spelled in that word:

pitcher	motor	sugar	river
dollar	together	remember	cellar
mirror	hammer	wonder	collar
color	another	doctor	summer

-er	-ar	-or

e. Spelling Pretest

f. Enrichment

Put a verb in the blanks to complete the sentences.

1) The dog ______________.

2) The cat ______________.

3) The mouse ______________.

4) The carpenter ______________.

5) The mother ______________.

6) The student ______________.

Day 5 a. – d. Discussion with teacher.

e. Spelling Test

______________ ______________

______________ ______________

______________ ______________

f. Enrichment

Fill in the blank with the word that comes next in the list.

1) small smaller ______________

2) quick quicker ______________

3) loud louder ______________

4) few more ______________

5) never sometimes ______________

6) dark darker ______________

g. Journal Entry: Complete this thought: On Saturdays I like to

______________.

h. Handwriting

When

Water

Went

Woke

What

1 2 3

Very

Vase

Visit

Vest

Van

1 2 3

Us

1 2 3

Under

Use

Upon

Uncle

Review Activities

1. Underline the actual words spoken or thought.

   a. "I wonder if Nick is home," thought Hunter.

   b. "I will ask Jason," he thought to himself.

   c. "Let's go see if Nick is home," said Jason.

   d. "Good idea!" replied Hunter.

2. Add the suffix **-ed** to these words.

   a. wash ______________________

   b. rally ______________________

   c. marry ______________________

   d. pat ______________________

   e. poke ______________________

3. Divide each word into syllables.

   a. difficult ______________________

   b. separate ______________________

   c. pretty ______________________

   d. literature ______________________

4. Make compound words by matching words from both lists.

some	pole
sun	night
tad	thing
good	card
post	shine

That one small victory made it easier to carry on. He paddled all the harder. The current was stronger now, the water deeper and moving faster.

The Tale of Jeremy Vole, Copyright 1990 by Stephen Lawhead. Published by Lion Publishing Corporation. All rights reserved. Used by permission.

Day 1 a. Write the literature passage from dictation, or copy it. Compare your copy to the model and make corrections.

b.

Focus on Spelling

current turn early learn hurry

Bonus Word: victory

Copy these spelling words. Say the words aloud as you write them.

c. Enrichment

Find your spelling words in the puzzle: current early hurry turn learn

t	u	r	n	o	c	b
i	e	a	r	l	y	a
t	l	e	a	r	n	l
h	t	w	a	r	o	o
c	u	r	r	e	n	t
y	h	u	r	r	y	g

d. Review your spelling words from Lessons 29 – 31.

Day 2 a. In this lesson underline the words with the suffix **-er** added.

b. Write down the adjectives you underlined and draw a line between **-er** and the base word. Look at the base word, or root word, and see if you think it is spelled correctly.

______________ ______________ ______________

______________ ______________ ______________

c. All the base words stayed the same except for *easier*. The base word is *easy*. Tell your teacher how the word *easy* was changed to add the suffix **-er**.

Grammar Guide

To add **-er** to a word ending in a consonant and **y**, change the **y** to **i** and add **-er**.

Add the suffix **-er** to each of these base words:

1) dirty ______________
2) dark ______________
3) dry ______________
4) small ______________
5) sick ______________
6) hungry ______________
7) quick ______________
8) heavy ______________

d. Fill in these sentences with one of the words you made in **2c**.

1) By dinner time she was ______________ than Mom.
2) The rabbit is ______________ than the turtle.
3) The night seems ______________ without the moon's light.
4) My piece of cake is ______________ than yours.
5) Luke feels so sick. He is ______________ than Gabe.
6) The sand is ______________ before it rains.
7) The boy is dirty, but the baby is ______________.
8) The couch is ______________ than the chair.

e. **SEE-SPELL-SAY:** Look and **see** each word on the spelling list. **Spell** each word aloud. **Say** the word.

Day 3 a. Do you think this is a true or make-believe story? Why do you think so?

____

____

b. Stories that are real or true are called **nonfiction** while stories that are make-believe are called **fiction**. Is our story fiction or nonfiction?

____

c. Discussion with teacher.

d. Write the names of your books into these spaces. Make sure you start the first word in each of the titles with a capital letter. Capitalize every other important word. Underline the title. Ex: <u>The Tale of Jeremy Vole</u>

Nonfiction Books

1) ______________________________
2) ______________________________
3) ______________________________

4) ______________________________

5) ______________________________

Fiction Books

1) ______________________________

2) ______________________________

3) ______________________________

4) ______________________________

5) ______________________________

e. Spelling Bee

f. Enrichment

Write an adjective describing each noun.

1) ____________ mice

2) ____________ horses

3) ____________ monkeys

4) ____________ day

5) ____________ floor

6) ____________ room

Day 4 a. Why do you think this is a victory for Jeremy?

____

____

b. Read the sentence to your teacher that tells how things are going for Jeremy.

c. Discussion with teacher.

d. On a separate piece of paper draw a picture (or pictures) of Jeremy and his struggles.

e. Spelling Pretest

______________________ ______________________

______________________ ______________________

______________________ ______________________

f. Enrichment

Look at the diagram and follow these directions.

A	**B**	**C**	**D**	**E**	**F**	**G**
H	**I**	**J**	**K**	**L**	**M**	**N**
O	**P**	**Q**	**R**	**S**	**T**	**U**
V	**W**	**X**	**Y**	**Z**	**1**	**2**

1) Start at D, go down 2, go right 1. Where are you? __________

2) Start at M, go left 3, go down 2. Where are you? __________

3) Start at G, go left 2, go down 2. Where are you? __________

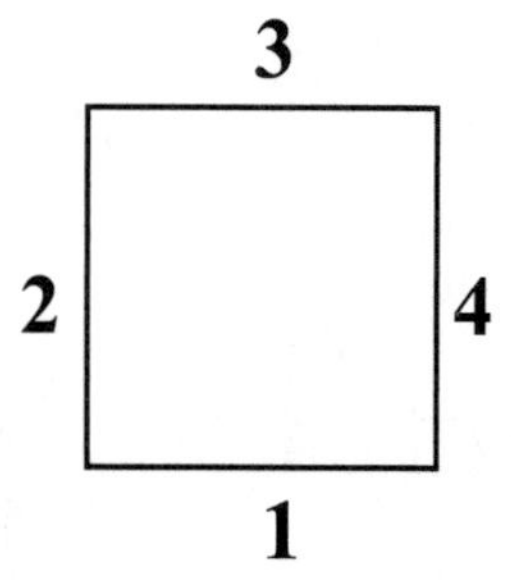

Look at this square. It is resting on side 1.

4) If you flip it one time to the left, which side would it rest on now? __________

5) If you put it resting on side 1 again, and flip it one time to the right, what side would it rest on? __________

6) If you put it resting on side 1 again, and flip it upside down, what side would it rest on? __________

Day 5 a. Discussion with teacher.

b. Spelling Test

c. Journal Entry: If you could visit any place in the world, where would you go? ______________________________

Explain why you choose this place.

d. Handwriting

X-ray

Xerox

Xenon

Xylophone

1 2 3 4

Yard

Yellow

You

Yummy

Yip

1 2 3

Zipper

Zero

Zoo

Review Activities

1. Add the suffix **-er** to these words.

   a. tall ________________

   b. messy ________________

   c. kind ________________

   d. slow ________________

   e. happy ________________

2. Write *fiction* or *nonfiction* to make these sentences true.

   a. A story that tells about something true is called ________________.

   b. A story that tells about something that is make-believe is called ________________________________.

3. Read each sentence and decide if it is fact or opinion.

   a. Vanilla ice cream is much better than chocolate. ________________

   b. We begin school at 10:00 am. ________________

   c. I use the computer for an hour every day. ________________

   d. *Where the Red Fern Grows* is the best story. ________________

4. Write the past tense of these irregular verbs.

   a. begin ________________

   b. bite ________________

   c. dig ________________

   d. do ________________

Assessment 7
(Lessons 29 – 32)

1. Underline the actual words spoken or thought.

   a. "I would like to go to the park," thought Justin.

   b. "Let's go to the park to play," said Mom.

   c. "Hurray! Let's go!" said Mark.

   d. "I'll pack a lunch," said Katie.

2. Add the suffix **-ed** to these words.

   a. wait ____________

   b. bury ____________

   c. shop ____________

   d. rake ____________

3. Add the suffix **-er** to these words.

   a. small ____________

   b. silly ____________

   c. cold ____________

   d. funny ____________

4. Circle the word spelled incorrectly in each group.

a. chief	beleive	field	piece
b. handle	settle	finel	uncle
c. noyse	spoil	boil	point

Notes

EVERYDAY WORDS

Day 1 a. Discussion with teacher.

b. Look over the story "Encyclopedia Brown and the Case of the Forgetful Sheriff." Make a list of any unfamiliar words.

Encyclopedia Brown and the Case of the Forgetful Sheriff

Led by Mr. Scotty, the party of eastern tourists rode the Texas range. The hotel manager had promised them "Historic Scenes of the Old Wild West." Who knew what another mile might bring?

Encyclopedia Brown knew. More blisters.

He rode last in line. Behind him came only the chuck wagon with the food. Around noon, even the chuck wagon passed him.

Encyclopedia didn't mind. It was lunch time.

Most of the tourists (including Encyclopedia) ate standing up. It made the boy detective mad to see his father sitting contentedly on the ground.

"You don't look well, Leroy," he said.

"I wish Bugs Meany were sitting in my place," said Encyclopedia.

Chief Brown grinned. "I had the cowboy at the hotel give you the gentlest horse in the stable."

"Then I must have the toughest saddle," answered Encyclopedia. "Say, Dad, do you think I made Mr. Scotty mad before?"

"No, but you upset him when you figured out the truth about the gunfight between Ringo Charlie and Johnny Kid," replied his father.

"I'll try to keep still," vowed Encyclopedia.

For the next half hour of riding there was little else to do. The horses plodded across flat grasslands. At last Mr. Scotty called, "Dismount here, folks."

The skinny little guide led the way to a pocket formed by nine high rocks.

"Now this here spot is called Outlaw Cemetery. It was so named on account of the five outlaws done in here eighty years ago," he began.

"Them outlaws held up the bank at River Falls. They escaped with twelve thousand dollars in gold," said Mr. Scotty.

"Sheriff Wiggins immediately set out after the desperadoes. But he was new on the job and forgetful. He forgot to put on his six-gun."

Mr. Scotty paused. He looked at the crowd of tourists to see if everyone was paying attention. He looked especially at Encyclopedia.

Then he resumed his tale.

"One of the citizens of River Falls happened to enter the sheriff's office. He saw the sheriff's six-gun still on the desk. Quickly he spread the word. A posse of citizens was rounded up to ride out and help the unarmed lawman capture the bank robbers. About ten miles out of town the posse heard gun play. When the shooting stopped, the posse rode up to this here spot. Stretched out dead as fish in a barrel were them five outlaws."

Mr. Scotty began hopping about as he warmed to his tale.

"Sheriff Wiggins," he said, "had recovered the stolen gold. But he was wounded in his left arm. In his modest way, he told the posse what had happened. He said the lookout for the outlaws saw him coming and shot two bullets into his left arm."

Suddenly Mr. Scotty clutched his left arm above the elbow. Then he made a leap and began to throw himself around.

"Sheriff Wiggins said he wrestled the lookout's pearl-handled six-gun away despite his wounded left arm. Then he shot the lookout with his own gun—a bullet through the heart it was."

At this point, Mr. Scotty dropped to one knee. "Right away the other four outlaws came at Sheriff Wiggins shooting up a storm," he said. "But the sheriff was cool as a hog on ice. He drilled them four desperadoes—*bang*! *bang*! *bang*! *bang*! in four seconds flat."

The skinny little guide jumped to his feet. He was breathing heavily with the effort of acting out the heroic sheriff's one-man stand against the five outlaws.

"The outlaws were buried on boothill," he continued. "The stolen gold was returned to the bank at River Falls.

Everybody in town claimed Sheriff Wiggins ought to run for president."

Mr. Scotty dusted himself off carefully, letting the tourists wait for more of the story.

Then he said, "The town gave a dinner for the sheriff, though he said he didn't deserve the honor. Why, he was only doing his duty getting back the stolen gold, he said. But Mr. Baker, the bank president, disagreed."

Again Mr. Scotty broke off his tale to look at the tourists. He shot Encyclopedia a sly glance. It seemed to say, "Ready to solve this one, sonny?"

"Mr. Baker," concluded Mr. Scotty, "said Sheriff Wiggins had done a mite more than his duty. And since this was the lawman's last meal, he'd better eat well. Then Mr. Baker said something that made the three biggest men at the dinner seize Sheriff Wiggins. Somebody got a rope, and at sunrise they hanged the lawman!"

The tourists gasped in amazement.

After a brief silence, a lady from Vermont asked,

"What did Mr. Baker say that made them hang the sheriff?"

"Why, now, that's the puzzle, isn't it?" replied Mr. Scotty, "I don't expect that anybody here could solve it, could he?"

The skinny little guide did not mention anyone by name. But the grown-ups on the tour turned and looked at Encyclopedia.

Chief Brown looked at him, too.

"Should I speak out, Dad?' asked Encyclopedia.

"If you know what Mr. Baker said that made the citizens hang Sheriff Wiggins," said his father.

Encyclopedia took a step forward. "Mr. Baker said that—"

WHAT DID MR. BAKER SAY?

Mr. Baker said:

"You can't shoot seven bullets from a six-gun."

Count them.

Sheriff Wiggins claimed: he was wounded in the left arm by two shots (two bullets) from the lookout's six-gun; he then seized the lookout's gun and killed him with it (three bullets); then he shot the remaining four outlaws (seven bullets!).

Encyclopedia reasoned (as had Mr. Baker) that the sheriff was secretly a member of the holdup gang. In riding after his outlaw partners, the lawman didn't bother to put on his gun because he didn't think he'd need it.

Then he had a falling out over the division of the loot, probably. Getting hold of a gun, he surprised and killed his partners.

Before he could ride off with the gold, the posse reached him. So he had to make up the story about shooting the five outlaws in the line of duty.

c. **Discussion Questions**

1) In what state does this story take place?
2) To what special place did the guide take the group?
3) What had outlaws stolen 80 years before? Who had chased after them?
4) What did Sheriff Wiggins forget?
5) What happened to the outlaws?
6) What did Sheriff Wiggins say happened?
7) What did Mr. Baker, the bank president, say?

d. Discussion with teacher.

Day 2 a. You have done several Word Search puzzles in this book. Complete these simple Word Searches to prepare you for the larger Word Search puzzle in **2d**.

R	C	B
L	A	M
E	T	S

b. This word was written from top to bottom. Some words are hidden from left to right (or side to side). Find the word *dog*, and circle it:

B	N	E
L	P	S
D	O	G

c. When you do a Word Search, often letters are shared by more than one word, like in a crossword puzzle. Here is an example. Find the words *big* and *bat*, and circle each word separately:

B	I	G
A	O	Z
T	L	Y

d. Now you are ready to find the following words in the Word Search puzzle. Here are your words to find. (Notice all the words and letters are capitals.)

Brown	Sheriff	Texas
Leroy	Gold	Horse
Sixgun	Bank	

B	U	Z	D	N	Y	A	C	K	J
R	J	F	P	H	O	R	S	E	M
O	G	E	C	S	F	L	Q	W	U
W	O	N	K	V	G	E	P	D	K
N	L	Q	S	H	E	R	I	F	F
S	D	W	I	P	D	O	C	L	Y
F	Y	J	X	M	F	Y	S	B	P
H	K	Z	G	U	T	E	X	A	S
V	D	I	U	L	A	J	H	N	V
A	C	P	N	R	S	W	Q	K	O

If you want to do more Word Searches there are many bookstores and grocery stores that have them.

Day 3 a. Another kind of word puzzle is called a letter number puzzle. Each letter in the alphabet is assigned a number. When you see each number you are to find the letter it represents in the key and write it on the line. After you write all the letters you should be able to read a word. Another word for this kind of puzzle is a code. Try this puzzle:

KEY							
A	B	C	D	E	F	G	H
7	3	1	2	5	8	6	9

____ ____ ____ ____ ____
3 5 7 1 9

b. Try to solve this puzzle:

KEY												
A	E	I	O	U	B	C	D	F	G	H	J	K
5	10	15	20	25	1	2	3	4	6	7	8	9

___ ___ ___ ___ ___ ___ ___ ___
5 1 15 6 2 5 9 10

c. Here is a coded message for you to figure out:

KEY										
B	C	D	F	G	H	J	K	L	M	N
6	7	8	9	10	11	12	13	14	15	16
P	Q	R	S	T	V	W	X	Y	Z	
17	18	19	20	21	22	23	24	25	26	
A	E	I	O	U						
1	2	3	4	5						

___   ___ ___ ___ ___   ___ ___
3   14 3 13 2   21 4

___ ___ ___ ___   ___ ___ ___ ___ ___
19 2 1 8   1 6 4 5 21

___ ___ ___ ___ ___ ___ ___ ___ ___ ___.
8 2 21 2 7 21 3 22 2 20

___ ___   ___ ___   ___ ___ ___
3 21   3 20   9 5 16

___ ___   ___ ___ ___ ___ ___   ___
21 4   20 4 14 22 2   1

___ ___ ___ ___ ___ ___ ___.
15 25 20 21 2 19 25

d. Discussion with teacher.

Day 4 a. A code is a kind of puzzle. Some codes are numbers, and some codes are letters. Another kind of code is called Morse code. It consists of dots and dashes. It was developed by Samuel Morse. Look at the copy of Morse code below.

A	•–	**M**	––	**Y**	–•––
B	–•••	**N**	–•	**Z**	––••
C	–•–•	**O**	–––	**1**	•––––
D	–••	**P**	•––•	**2**	••–––
E	•	**Q**	––•–	**3**	•••––
F	••–•	**R**	•–•	**4**	••••–
G	––•	**S**	•••	**5**	•••••
H	••••	**T**	–	**6**	–••••
I	••	**U**	••–	**7**	––•••
J	•–––	**V**	•••–	**8**	–––••
K	–•–	**W**	•––	**9**	––––•
L	•–••	**X**	–••–	**0**	–––––

b. Try to decode the following message:

– •••• •   –••• •• ––•   –•–• •– •–•

___ ___ ___   ___ ___ ___   ___ ___ ___

•• •••   •–• • –••

___ ___   ___ ___ ___.

c. Try to decode the following phrases:

–•–• ––– –– •

___ ___ ___ ___

––– •••– • •–•   – –––

___ ___ ___ ___   ___ ___

–– –•––   •••• ––– ••– ••• •

___ ___   ___ ___ ___ ___ ___.

d. Review spelling words in Lessons 29 – 32.

Day 5 a. Spelling

b. Dictation

1)

2)

c. Discussion with teacher.

1)

2)

d. I have wheels, but I often go for walks.
I carry someone special who someday will be able to push me around. What am I?

e. Riddles can be about many different things. Here are some more riddles for you to solve:

1) I have a face and two hands, but I can not see.
What am I?

____

2) I can be tall or small. I always have to stand. I have a lot of bark, but no bite!
What am I?

____

3) I can hold water, or I can throw a baseball.
What am I?

____

f. Here are some more riddles about things. See if you can guess what the answers are:

1) I am white and puffy. I am used to being up high.
What am I?

____

2) I go up white and come down yellow.
What am I?

____

3) You can throw me and catch me. You can kick me and hold me, but you can't roll me in a straight line.
What am I?

____

4) I have legs, but I can't walk. I often have leaves. I am made of wood, but I am not a tree.
What am I?

5) I often have a tongue, but I can't talk. Most people wouldn't leave home without me, though I do get kicked around a lot.
What am I?

6) I can be skinny one minute and ready to pop the next. I go to all the best parties though people say I'm full of air.
What am I?

g. Now you try to write your own riddles. Riddles are usually three or four lines long. The first two or three lines are clues, and the last line is "What am I?" or "Who am I?"

h. Handwriting

1 3 2 Randy

Robert

Rest

Run

1 3 2 Best

Boat

Bike

Back

1 2 Kind

Key

Know

Keep

Park

Plan

Pie

Put

Pledge of Allegiance

I pledge allegiance to the flag, of the United States of America, and to the Republic for which it stands, one nation under God, indivisible, with liberty and justice for all.

Day 1 a. Copy the Pledge of Allegiance. Compare your copy to the one in this lesson and make corrections.

b. Enrichment

Write an adjective in each blank to describe the noun.

1) ______________________ fire

2) ______________________ star

3) ______________________ moon

4) ______________________ hat

5) ______________________ shoe

6) ______________________ jacket

Day 2 a. – c. Discussion with teacher.

d. Enrichment

You are going grocery shopping. Find at least one thing for each letter of the word, *groceries*.
Ex: G – gum, R – radishes, etc.

G ____________________

R ____________________

O ____________________

C ____________________

E ____________________

R ____________________

I ____________________

E ____________________

S ____________________

Day 3 a. – b. There are many large, but important, words in our pledge. Read through the pledge with your teacher and make a list of the words for which you do not know the meaning. Look up these words in the dictionary and write their meanings.

____

____

____

c. Discussion with teacher.

d. Enrichment

Using the letters in the word *encyclopedia*, write as many words as you can.

E N C Y C L O P E D I A

E ____________________

N ____________________

C ____________________

Y ____________________

C ____________________

L ____________________

O ____________________

P ____________________

E ____________________

D ____________________

I ____________________

A ____________________

Day 4 a. Where did we get the Pledge of Allegiance and why do we say it? With your teacher's assistance look up the "Pledge of Allegiance" on the Internet.

b. Write a paragraph on the Pledge of Allegiance. Tell when it was written and by whom. Give all other information you find interesting. Write down your information in complete sentences, not as a list.

____

____

____

____

c. Discussion with teacher.

d. You are now going to review the spelling words presented in Lessons 1 – 15. Read over these spelling words.

Lesson 1
knot
know
knee
knife
knock
BW – because

Lesson 2
every
everybody
everyone
everything
everywhere
BW – clothes

Lesson 3
feel
keep
wheel
seen
need
BW – really

Lesson 4
pray
crayon
holiday
stay
gray
BW – were

Lesson 7
through
group
mouth
count
ground
BW – always

Lesson 8
yellow
swallow
shadow
follow
pillow
BW – perhaps

Lesson 9
beach
treat
clean
peace
leave
BW – sincerely

Lesson 10
some
somebody
something
sometimes
somewhere
BW – night

Lesson 11
dirty
third
girl
bird
first
BW – along

Lesson 12
wear
year
clear
hear
dear
BW – queen

Lesson 13
sail
wait
plain
raise
hair
BW – tomorrow

Lesson 15
who
what
when
where
why
BW – reporter

e. Use a yellow highlighter pen (or a yellow crayon or colored pencil) to mark any words that seem hard to you. You may also want to ask your teacher which words you may have had trouble with before. Use your **SEE-SPELL-SAY** process to practice any words that give you trouble.

Day 5 a. Spelling Test

1. ____________________
2. ____________________
3. ____________________
4. ____________________
5. ____________________

6. ____________________
7. ____________________
8. ____________________
9. ____________________
10. ____________________

11. ____________________
12. ____________________
13. ____________________
14. ____________________
15. ____________________

16. ____________________
17. ____________________
18. ____________________
19. ____________________
20. ____________________

b. Enrichment

Read the list of words in the word box. Write the correct verb under each picture.

Word Box
sit jump read slide

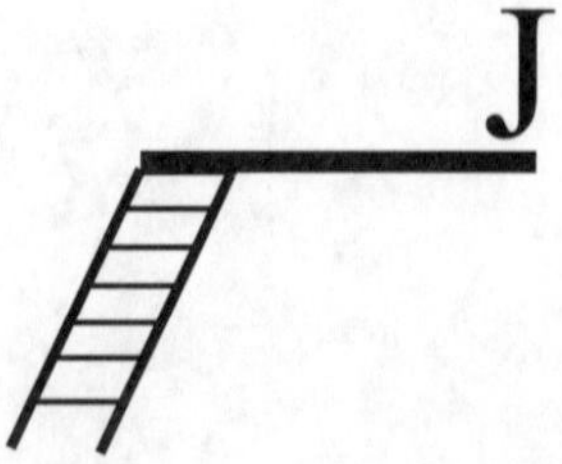

Word Box
sing cry shout ride

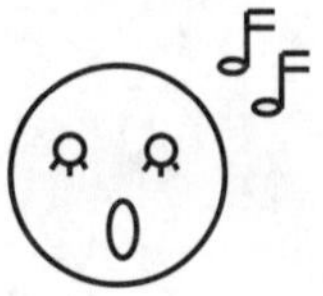

c. Journal Entry: List places where you have seen the National flag.

d. Handwriting

Lake

Look

Late

Lunch

The

Take

Tool

Turn

Trick

1 2
5
4
3
Fast

Food

Fun

Fix

Fence

Review Activities

1. Write the words in each list in alphabetical order.

a. party balloon candles gifts

____

____

____

____

b. flag friend fall forest

____

____

____

____

c. nation navy name nail

____

____

____

____

2. Add quotation marks and capitalization to the sentences.

a. noah asked can we go to the farm soon

____

b. we can go as soon as we eat lunch said mom

____

c. sarah replied I cannot wait to see the horses

____

3. Combine the words to form contractions.

a. he is ____________

b. would have ____________

c. she will ____________

d. they have ____________

4. Circle the articles and underline the nouns.

a. The boy ran a mile in the race.

b. A big, brown bear was on the hill.

c. We like blueberries in the muffins.

d. An old car sat in the driveway.

"Saint George and the Dragon"

Dragon: (roaring onto the stage) *I am the dragon, be afraid of my claws! I am the dragon, be afraid of my jaws!* (Dragon storms around the stage)

(King and Princess Enter)

King: *This dragon has no heart. He says he'll rip our land apart. (wringing his hands) Oh, dear, me, where can we flee?*

Princess: *My father, to save our land, my life I'll give. Here I stand.*

George: (running onto the stage) *Fair lady, do not fear. No dragon will harm you while I am near!*

(George and the Dragon fight)

Day 1 a. Copy the play. Compare your copy to the play and make corrections.

b. Enrichment

Using the letters in the word *Washington*, write as many words as you can.

W A S H I N G T O N

W

A

S

H

I

N

G

T

O

N

Day 2 a. Here is a list of commonly used pronouns. Read them to your teacher.

Pronouns								
I	me	you	he	she	they	me	his	mine
him	her	it	we	us	them	my		

b. Using this list underline all the pronouns in our play, and tell your teacher what noun each one replaced.

c. Use the correct pronoun to replace the italicized words:

1) *John* is in bed. ________________ is in bed.

2) Please give it to *Rachel*. Please give it to ____________.

3) *Isaac and Will* are playing football. ____________ are playing football.

4) *Mother and I* like to cook. ____________ like to cook.

5) *The car* is green. ________________ is green.

6) The bag belongs to *Ann*. The bag belongs to __________.

d. Make up four sentences about family members. Use their names in each sentence. Then rewrite each sentence replacing the names with pronouns. Ex: *Mother* and *Jeff* are going to church. *They* are going to church.

____

____

____

____

____

____

____

____

____

e. Enrichment

Using a clock or watch, write down how long it takes you to do each of the following.

1) Count from 1 to 100. __________

2) Flip a coin and get heads ten times. __________

3) Hop on one foot with your arms held in front of you. __________

4) Say the alphabet. ________

5) Count from 100 backwards to 1. ________

Day 3 a. Using a red pencil underline the stage directions.

b. Using a blue pencil underline only what the character named Dragon says. Using a green pencil underline only what the King says. Using a pink pencil underline what the Princess says. Using a yellow pencil underline what George says.

c. Rewrite what the Dragon said by making it into a sentence with quotation marks. Put the first quotation mark before his actual words begin, and put the closing quotation mark after his last word and period. Remember to leave out stage directions.

d. Do the same thing with the words of the other characters. Write his or her words as a sentence using quotation marks.

e. Review the four types of sentences you learned about in Lesson 19, Day 3. Find an example of each type of sentence in this week's play. Read them to your teacher.

Day 4 a. – b. Discussion with Teacher

c. On a separate piece of paper, continue writing the play from Day 1 using the story you've just heard. Remember to write it in play form.

d. You are going to review the spelling words presented in Lessons 17 – 32. Read over these spelling words.

Lesson 17
please
pleased
pleasing
grow
growing
BW – jungle

Lesson 19
thought
bought
brought
fought
ought
BW – would

Lesson 20
write
wrap
wreck
wrote
wrong
BW – happened

Lesson 24
right
bright
light
night
might
BW – wonderful

Lesson 25
morning
evening
sunrise
sunset
sunshine
BW – Sunday

Lesson 26
winter
summer
spring
garden
season
BW – fruit

Lesson 27
head
dead
bread
instead
ready
BW – pleasant

Lesson 29
noise
spoil
point
coin
boil
BW – difficult

Lesson 30
new
glue
tool
soup
flew
BW – juice

Lesson 31
chief
believe
field
piece
yield
BW – finally

Lesson 32
current
turn
early
learn
hurry
BW – victory

e. Discussion with teacher.

Day 5 a. – b. Discussion with teacher.

1. ____________
2. ____________
3. ____________
4. ____________
5. ____________
6. ____________
7. ____________
8. ____________
9. ____________
10. ____________
11. ____________
12. ____________
13. ____________
14. ____________
15. ____________
16. ____________
17. ____________
18. ____________
19. ____________
20. ____________

c. Enrichment

Circle the correct answer.

1) A penpal is visiting you from another country. He says to you, "Let's play. I will get a **thlimper**."

   Do you think **thlimper** is a kind of toy, a number, or something to eat?

2) "I will teach you how to sew. Do you have a **koomp and klump**?"

   Do you think **koomp and klump** is bacon and eggs, bat and ball, or needle and thread?

3) "I want to mail this letter. I need a **zimfer**."

   Do you think a **zimfer** is a zipper, button, or stamp?

4) "I cut my finger. Do you have a **dunker**?"

   Do you think a **dunker** is a pen, donut, or bandage?

5) "We can't reach the apples. Let's get a **flump**."

   Do you think a **flump** is a flashlight, ladder, or cup?

6) "The sun has been shining all day. I am so **shlomp**."

   Do you think **shlomp** means hungry, hot, or worried?

7) "The stairs are broken. Be **poshle**!"

   Do you think **poshle** means happy, careful, or late?

8) "The hairy **fungu** crawled into the bushes."

   Do you think **fungu** is a type of ball, an animal, or something to eat?

9) "I am very tired. Where is a **shlacky**?"

   Do you think **shlacky** is a type of game, an animal, or a bed?

10) "I need a **zoogla**. It is raining."

    Do you think **zoogla** is something to eat, an animal, or something to wear?

d. Journal Entry: Explain how to play one of your favorite games.

e. Handwriting

Jump

Jack

Jill

June

Ice

I'm

I'll

If

Dave

Date

Done

Did

1
2
Egg

Every

Eat

Eye

Review Activities

1. Replace the underlined words with pronouns.

   a. Dad and I went fishing.

   ____

   ____

   b. Dad caught four big fish.

   ____

   ____

   c. Dad's friend let us use the boat.

   ____

   ____

   d. The trip was fun.

   ____

   ____

2. Add quotation marks to these sentences.

   a. Seth said, Emily is here.

   b. Come home soon, said Mom.

   c. I am so hungry, thought James.

A wise old owl sat in an oak.
The more he heard, the less he spoke;
The less he spoke, the more he heard.
Why aren't we all like that wise old bird?

Mother Goose Rhyme

Day 1 a. Write the poem from dictation, or copy it. Compare your copy to the poem and make corrections.

b. Enrichment

Complete these analogies. Review earlier lessons if needed.

1) round : ball :: square : ______
2) duck : quack :: turkey : ______
3) teacher : student :: doctor : ______
4) Jennifer : she :: Tommy : ______
5) Jim and I : we :: Jim and Tom : ______
6) Kim's : her :: Tom's : ______
7) snout : pig :: trunk : ______
8) thumb : hand :: toe : ______
9) knee : leg :: elbow : ______

10) least : most :: less : ____________________

11) see : saw :: hear : ____________________

12) stand : stood :: sit : ____________________

13) tall : short :: foolish : ____________________

14) blue and red : purple :: yellow and blue : ____________

15) white and black : gray :: white and red : ____________

Day 2 a. Underline the words in our poem that show past tense.

b. Point out each underlined word for your teacher and tell her the word which shows the action happening now.
Ex: slept – sleep gave – give

sat ____________ heard ____________ spoke ____________

c. Match the following words with their irregular past tenses:

make	said
see	made
do	left
tell	saw
say	did
leave	told

d. Play Verb Tense Match-up.

Day 3 a. Circle the words **a** and **an** in the poem. These words tell you that a noun is coming.

b. Write the article which comes before *oak*. 1) ____________ oak

Write the article which comes before *wise old owl*. 2) ____ wise old owl

c. Look at this list and see if you can think of a rule that might tell you when to use *a* and when to use *an*:

an apple a car a bat a dog an egg an umbrella

d. Write *a* or *an* in each blank:

1) I will get ______________ ice cream cone.

2) Brycen and Jon are going on ______________ boat ride.

3) Dad will catch ______________ fish today.

4) Mom gave us ______________ orange for our snack.

5) ______________ animal ran by the pond.

6) We will get ______________ dog for a pet.

e. Enrichment

1) Jill is older than Sarah, but younger than Traci. List the children in order from youngest to oldest.

______________ ______________ ______________

2) Katy is shorter than Jessica. Brandi is shorter than Katy. List the children in order from shortest to tallest.

______________ ______________ ______________

3) Kim is faster than Ashley. Ashley is faster than Emily. Emily is faster than Tonya. Who is the fastest girl?

____

Day 4 a. What do you think makes this owl wise?

____

____

b. – d. Discussion with teacher.

e. Enrichment

List the words you might hear on a fishing trip.

List the words you might hear while preparing dinner at home.

Day 5 a. Handwriting

Some

Safe

Sweet

Sure

Side

Sleep

1 2 3 Great

Good

Girl

Game

Get

Grandma

Review Activities

1. Write the past tense of these verbs. Show that the action already happened.

a. tell ______________ c. leave ______________

b. say ______________ d. do ______________

2. Write the article *a* or *an* in the blanks.

a. __________ old goat

b. __________ happy boy

c. __________ snake

d. __________ alligator

3. Divide each word into syllables.

a. baseball ______________ c. already ______________

b. alligator ______________ d. irregular ______________

4. Replace the names with the correct pronoun.

a. Ryan and Noah went to the farm.

____

b. Sarah, Abi, and I ate popcorn today.

____

c. Joe was at the farm yesterday.

____

d. Leanna likes to bake cookies.

____

Assessment 8
(Lessons 33 – 36)

1. Add quotation marks and capitalization to these sentences.

   a. May Leanna come to the party asked Abi.

   b. Yes. She may come, replied Mom.

   c. Mom said you may ask Skye also.

   d. Abi cried, we will have so much fun! I can hardly wait!

2. Replace the underlined words with pronouns.

   a. <u>Jason</u> likes baseball. __________ plays well.

   b. <u>Jason and Mike</u> are the best players on our team. __________ play well.

   c. <u>Laura and I</u> play piano. __________ like it.

   d. <u>Laura</u> has been playing since she was six years old. __________ is very good.

3. Write the past tense of these verbs. Show that the action has already happened.

   a. see ________________

   b. make ________________

   c. leave ________________

   d. tell ________________

4. Write the articles *a* or *an* in the blanks.

   a. I need __________ drink of water.

   b. I will eat __________ apple.

   c. I saw __________ ape at the zoo.

   d. The cat chased __________ mouse.

APPENDIX

Materials for Lessons

Punctuation Pointers

Grammar Guides

Phonics Facts

Using Your Tools

Focus on Writing

Bibliography

Lesson 13 – **4 c**

	Nouns	
car	boat	rain
night	sky	dog
baby	candy	hat
fish		
	Adjectives	
dark	new	old
black	red	loud
hot	quiet	slow
big		

Lesson 26 – **5 a – b**

dog	car	box
boy	door	tree
book	coat	hat
flower	house	truck
sun	toy	girl
cat	table	bench
bed	ball	
smart	pretty	fuzzy
hard	old	friendly
hot	round	soft
blue	loud	cold
red	tall	heavy
noisy	big	green
fast	wooden	torn

Lesson 26 - **5 a-b**

noun	noun	noun
noun	noun	noun
noun	noun	noun
noun	noun	noun
noun	noun	noun
noun	noun	noun
noun	noun	noun
adjective	adjective	adjective
adjective	adjective	adjective
adjective	adjective	adjective
adjective	adjective	adjective
adjective	adjective	adjective
adjective	adjective	adjective
adjective	adjective	adjective

Lesson 26 - **5 a-b** con't

small	open	slow
fun	broken	happy
long	new	pink

Lesson 32 – **5a**

1. taller	1. shorter	
2. faster	2. slower	
3. harder	3. softer	
4. drier	4. wetter	
5. cleaner	5. dirtier	
6. darker	6. lighter	
7. sooner	7. later	
8. louder	8. quieter	
9. bigger	9. smaller	
10. happier	10. sadder	

Lesson 26 - **5 a-b** con't

adjective	adjective	adjective
adjective	adjective	adjective
adjective	adjective	adjective

Lesson 36 - **2d**

think	thought	make
made	feel	felt
eat	ate	buy
bought	do	did
pay	paid	come
came	sleep	slept
see	saw	begin
began	sit	sat
sing	sang	tell
told	keep	kept
hear	heard	have
had	say	said
take	took	speak
spoke	is	was

Lesson 36 - **2d** con't

leave	left	find
found	meet	met

Punctuation Pointers

1. **Period** - (**.**) ends a telling sentence
2. **Apostrophe** - (**'**) replaces missing letter(s) in a contraction
3. **Apostrophe** - Use an apostrophe **s** (**'s**) to show that something belongs to something or someone.
4. **Colon** - A colon (**:**) is used in a play after a character's name and before his lines.
5. **Quotation mark -** marks placed around the actual spoken word.

Grammar Guides

1. **Noun** - person, place, thing, or idea

2. **Proper noun** - name of a particular person, place, or thing. Proper nouns are spelled with a capital letter.

3. **Synonym** - a word of similar meaning

4. To add the suffix **-ing** or **-ed** to a word ending in silent **e**, first drop the **e**, and then add the suffix.
   Ex: bake - baking, baked

5. To add the suffix **-ing** or **-ed** to a one syllable word ending with a short vowel and a consonant, double the last consonant, and then add the suffix.
   Ex: stop - stopping, stopped

6. **Compound Word** - two words joined together to make a new word

7. When adding the suffix **-ed** to words ending in a consonant and **y**, first change the **y** to **i**, and then add **-ed**.
   Ex: worry - worried

8. To add the suffix **-ing** to words ending in **y**, just add **-ing**.
   Ex: play - playing   worry - worrying

9. When adding the suffix **-ed** and **-ing** to all other words, just add the suffix.
   Ex: help - helped - helping
   leak - leaked - leaking

10. **Contractions** - two words joined together with an apostrophe to replace missing letter(s)

11. **Conjunction** - a word that joins words or sentences

12. **Verb** - a doing word

13. **Antonym** - a word of opposite meaning

14. **Adjective** - a word that describes a person, place, or idea.

15. **Singular** - one
    Plural - more than one

16. If a word end with a consonant and **y**, change the **y** to **i** and add **es**.

17. **Singular possessive noun** - a singular noun with an apostrophe **s** (**'s**) to show that something belongs to something or someone

18. **Plural possessive noun** - a plural noun with an apostrophe (') to show that something belongs to something or someone

19. A **proper noun** names a particular person, place, or thing. Begin a proper noun with a **capital letter.**

20. To add **-er** to most words, just add **-er**. To add **-er** to a word ending with a silent **e**, drop the **e** and add **-er**.

21. **Pronoun** - a word which takes place of a noun

22. Begin the first word of a quotation with a **capital letter.**

23. **Complete sentence** - expresses a complete thought

24. **Subject** - tells who or what the sentence is about

25. **Predicate** - tells something about the subject

26. **Article** - a small word that tells you a noun is coming: *a* *an* *the*

27. **Adverb** - a word that describes a verb, an47 adjective, or another adverb

28. To add **-er** to a word ending in a consonant and **y**, change the **y** to **i** and add **-er**.

Phonics Facts

1. **kn** at the beginning of a word says /**n**/
2. When **gh** follows **i** the **gh** is silent, and **i** says /**i**/.
3. The letters **-le** at the end of a word will usually form its own syllable with the consonant before it.
4. The vowel before **-ng** usually says its short sound.
5. **Syllable** - part of a word which has a single vowel sound
6. **-tion** says /**shun**/
7. **-ed** at the end of a word can say /**ed**/ as in *pointed*, /**t**/ as in *boxed*, and /**d**/ as in *yelled*
8. The letters **-le**, **-el**, and **-al** at the end of a word say /**l**/.

Using Your Tools

1. A **thesaurus** is a book of synonyms listed in alphabetical order.

2. The **encyclopedia** is a book or set of books that contains information on various topics.

3. The **newspaper** gives you current events, weather, sports, and much more.

4. A **map** is a picture that shows the location of things and places.

Focus on Writing

1. A **paragraph** is a group of sentences that tell about one **main idea**. **Indent** the first sentence of a paragraph.

2. A **friendly letter** consists of a heading, greeting, body, closing, and signature.

3. A **simile** compares two things by using the words *like* or *as*.
   Ex: hungry as a lion
   swims like a fish

Bibliography

Bemelman, Ludwig. *Madeline*. 1939. Penguin Group.

Carroll, Lewis. *Alice's Adventures in Wonderland.*. 1865. Penguin Classics.

Dalgliesh, Alice. *The Courage of Sarah Noble*. 1954. Simon & Schuster.

Heilbroner, Joan. *Meet George Washington*. 1964. Random House.

Kipling, Rudyard. *The Jungle Book.* 1893. AmazonClassics.

Lawhead, Stephen. *The Tale of Jeremy Vol*e. 2003. Independently published.

Potter, Beatrix. *The Tale of Benjamin Bunny*. 1995. Warne

Shub, Elizabeth. *The White Stallion*. Random House.

St. John, Patricia. *The Other Kitt*en. 1990. Bethany House.

Notes